JACK SANFORD

FROM BLIGHTVILLE TO THE BIG LEAGUES

JIM HAWKINS

FOREWORD BY LUIS TIANT

PROLOGUE BY SAM MCDOWELL

3 SWALLYS PRESS
BOSTON, MASSACHUSETTS, USA

To Mom, whose unconditional love, support, and sacrifice was the glue that kept our family together.
—Laura, John, Nancy, and Susan

Acknowledgments

The author would like to thank John Sanford, who was determined to preserve his dad's remarkable story for posterity, and Jack's daughters, Laura, Nancy, and Susan, who, along with relatives and friends Jim Sanford, Phil Reynolds, Jeff DeCiccio, and Bill Blagg, graciously shared their memories and observations.

Thanks also to sportswriters Harry T. Paxton ("Baseball's Oldest Youngster," *Saturday Evening Post*, March 29, 1958), Bill Libby ("Jack Sanford's Grim World," *Sport*, March 1963), and the many others who preceded me in exploring this subject.

Finally, a book like this would not be possible without the remarkable resources of the Internet baseball bible, Baseball-Reference.com.

Contents

Foreword by Luis Tiant   *ix*

Prologue by Sam McDowell   *xiii*

1. Surprise!   *1*

2. Struggle and Perseverance   *7*

3. School of Hard Knocks   *20*

4. "I Had to Creep Up the Hard Way"   *34*

5. "One Good Year Doesn't Convince Me"   *50*

6. "Worst Trade I Ever Made"   *68*

7. "I've Won Twenty!"   *77*

8. "I Lost. That's All. I Just Lost"   *91*

9. "No Regrets, None Whatsoever"   *114*

10. Better a Has-Been than a Never-Was   *130*

Jack's Stats   *153*

Foreword

Luis Tiant was a journeyman right-handed pitcher who, in the first four years of his major league baseball career with the Cleveland Indians, had never won more than 12 games in a season. Then, in 1968, Jack Sanford, whose own playing career had recently ended, became the pitching coach of the Indians.

Immediately, under Sanford's tutelage, Tiant, a Cuban refugee who had a reputation for fading on the mound late in the season, became an All-Star and the ace of the Indians staff, winning 21 games and leading the American League with a career-best 1.60 earned-run average in 1968.

That season, Tiant also led the league with nine shutouts, four of them tossed in a row, and struck out a career-high 264 enemy batters, including 19 in one game. He did not allow a single runner to steal a base against him all year—a remarkable feat, considering the 258 innings he pitched.

In August, Sanford promised Tiant that if Luis won 20 games Jack would buy champagne for the entire team.

"I told him, 'Then I'll collect,' " Tiant declared. And he did.

To this day, Tiant, now 75, after a 19-year big league career that included 229 wins and was deemed worthy of significant Hall of Fame consideration, credits Jack Sanford with his turnaround and success.

~

Jack Sanford was a great man and a great friend. He became like a brother to me.

He helped me a lot with my pitching. He talked to me all the time, talking about the game. He would say, "I think you should change this," and "I think you should do that." He taught me a lot and we became very close. He was one of the best pitching coaches I ever had in my career.

Coming from Cuba, I didn't speak such good English. But Jack stuck with me. You can tell when somebody really wants to help you. Those are the people you listen to. Those are the people you get close to.

I had heard about Jack when he was playing with San Francisco. I knew he was a tough guy, the way he pitched. When he was pitching, he was a bad man.

I was tough, too. I pitched the way he used to pitch. We had similar styles. That was the kind of pitcher I wanted to be.

And Jack was a good pitcher. He gave me a lot of advice from all his years of pitching. He talked to me about how to go about my business. He told me, "Don't worry too much about the other guy. You have to mind your own business. You have to do your own thing."

He watched me. He watched me pitch. And he told me to stick with what I had and do what I had to do. He said, "Just do your job." He helped me a lot with my confidence.

Somebody can tell you what to do, but you still have to do it. You can talk to somebody, you can listen, you can remember what they tell you to do, but it's all up to you. You're the one out there on the mound. But I knew Jack wasn't just talking. He had done it.

After I got traded to Minnesota in 1969, I didn't see Jack for a long time. The last time I talked to him he was working at a golf course, a teaching pro. I called him because I had heard he was looking for me. After that, we talked two or three more times. Then I heard he had passed away.

I don't know why we didn't have more communication through the years. I wish we had. Because Jack Sanford meant a lot to me.

—Luis Tiant
November 2015

Prologue

Sam McDowell pitched in the major leagues for 15 years, mostly for the Cleveland Indians, and struck out 2,453 batters. Famed for his blazing fastball, McDowell's strikeout rate of 8.858 batters per nine innings pitched still ranks as the 12th best all-time.

In 1968, under the tutelage of Indians pitching coach Jack Sanford, McDowell won 15 games with an earned-run average of 1.81 and struck out 283 enemy batters to lead the American League. The next season, McDowell won 18 games and again led the AL in strikeouts with 279.

Following the 1969 season, when Sanford retired, McDowell offered to give Jack a portion of his $65,000-a-year salary if Sanford would stick around and continue to coach him.

Contrary to the prevailing perception that McDowell got his nickname "Sudden Sam" from fellow ballplayers because his famed fastball "suddenly" arrived at home plate, the moniker actually originated with sportswriter Bob Dolgan of the Cleveland Plain Dealer *during spring training in 1961.*

"*I did not get the idea from another ballplayer, another writer, a coach, or anybody else,*" recalled Dolgan, who at the time was a rookie baseball writer trying to impress his colleagues and editors and to make a name for himself. "*I made it up myself.*"

The character of Sam Malone, the alcoholic ex–Red Sox pitcher-turned-bar-owner portrayed by Emmy Award-winning actor Ted Danson in the television show "Cheers," was based on McDowell's baseball career.

~

Jack Sanford: From Blightville to the Big Leagues answers numerous questions we, as players, all had when Jack was our coach. He never talked about his career no matter what questions we had. And a coach's past is important to the players he's coaching. It shouldn't be, but all players will look up a coach's background.

As to Jack as our pitching coach, I will say, unequivocally, that Jack made me a major league pitcher.

Let me explain it this way. Even today, 99 percent of all coaches will always work on "mechanics." No matter what the problem, the coach will always talk about follow-through. Your step, your turn, arm angle, drawback, loading your system for delivery, and so on.

Mechanics were never my problem. I had a dad who taught me the perfect windup and delivery, the perfect way to throw a curve, slider, and changeup. I had, at the time, what were considered the best fastball, curve, slider, and changeup in the big leagues, but I couldn't win. I couldn't pitch in the majors.

No matter who my pitching coach was before Jack, it was always "mechanics."

Ironically, Birdie Tebbetts, who was referred to as the great psychologist/manager (as he took some psychology courses in college), would always say, "Just follow my instructions and I'll make you a great pitcher." Over and over when I would ask Birdie for answers, he would blow me off as if I wouldn't understand and again say just follow my instructions! Then all he would do is call every one of my pitches. With all the catchers he had signs and the catchers were allowed to call anything on their own. In the beginning I went along with the plan, but kept getting my ass kicked by even the worst hitters.

When Joe Adcock took over as manager, it was the same thing—calling all my pitches, and my getting my ass kicked!

Later on, after my career, it used to become a good laugh whenever I'd run into Jim Fregosi, as he would continually tell me they would just watch Birdie or Joe and know in advance what was coming when they got to the plate for their time at bat.

When Alvin Dark got hired as our manager and he hired Jack Sanford, the very first day of spring training they brought me into their office and Alvin explained, "Sam, we know all about Birdie and Joe calling all your pitches and we're not going to do that. You're going to become a pitcher and that's why I hired Jack."

From that day forward you might say I became a pitcher!

Ever since I first climbed the mound when I was eight years old, I simply tried to outguess the hitter. A little bit as an amateur, but the more I got hit in the majors, the more I began guessing, until some games I probably guessed 90 percent of my pitches.

From the first day I met Jack, he worked with me on the science of pitching. That is, why I throw each pitch, where I throw each pitch, how to set up the following pitch, why I want a groundball, when I want a fly ball, how to set up inside pitches, how to set up outside pitches, why you throw the up-and-in pitch for the following low-and-away pitches, and so on. The focus was always on controlling the hitter and the situation by focusing on my pitches, position, and what I should expect from the hitter if I do what I'm supposed to do.

Jack would sit next to me on the bench each game, and after each inning, go over what I did wrong the previous inning, what's coming up, and who the coming hitters will be. Never in a reprimanding manner, but an educational and compassionate manner. Perhaps a side of Jack that only I know. Bottom line, he made me a major league pitcher.

As many knew, I loved to drink. Basically the night

after I pitched I'd go out and get blitzed. The next night after the game I'd go out and get blitzed. Then the next two days I'd eat and drink healthy stuff, getting ready for my next start. Alvin Dark knew this and had Jack go out with me to protect me, as I was known to be a nasty drunk, getting into fights all the time. During these times Jack would continue discussing the game and all the good that happened and the things I needed to address. Then Jack would go back to the hotel to sleep and I'd continue on.

Although I thought it was confidential, as I knew the rules and ethics, when I heard Jack was thinking of retiring and going into golf, I did offer him some of my salary if he would stay as my coach. Basically whatever he would ask of me.

I not only respected Jack as the best coach I ever had, but I also loved the man. He was the most intelligent person I knew in terms of understanding pitching and the ability to explain it. I truly missed him when he left.

—Sam McDowell
June 2016

On May 18, 1999, more than three decades after Jack Sanford stepped onto a major league pitcher's mound with a baseball in hand for the final time, the talented, tormented former big league star reached the benchmark age of 70.

To celebrate the milestone, Jack's son, successful golf course architect John Sanford, decided to throw a surprise birthday party for his dad, who, outside of his family and circle of friends, was so often underappreciated or misunderstood. It was going to be a grand affair, a fitting tribute to the best baseball player that the affluent city of Wellesley, Massachusetts, has ever produced. Dozens of Jack's friends and golfing buddies gathered for the festivities. Although no one knew it at the time, it would be Jack's last birthday.

Jack Sanford had spent 12 years throwing fastballs in the big leagues without, at least in his friends' and family's opinion, ever receiving the accolades and acclaim that his career and his accomplishments deserved.

"In my mind," declared Jack's nephew Jim Sanford, who admittedly idolized his uncle, "he was the best baseball player who ever played."

Consider this: In the history of major league baseball, which dates back to 1869, fewer than 20,000 men—out of the hundreds of millions who have hoped and dreamed and tried—have proven themselves talented or lucky enough to play the grand old game at its highest level. Only a fraction of those 20,000 were gifted and fortunate enough to survive the rigors of the big leagues for a dozen grueling years, as Jack did. Even fewer had the patience and perseverance to labor for seven long years in the oblivion of the minor leagues before they finally reached baseball's promised land.

Unlike other professional sports, baseball's devotion to statistics allows its fans to compare the game's undisputed immortals with the unheralded from over more than a century of play. And, in the entire history of major league baseball, only one pitcher has ever won his league's Rookie of the Year Award, led his league in strikeouts, led his league in regular season starts, and started three games in a single World Series.

Only one.

That singular pitcher's name is not Hall of Famer Tom Seaver or sudden sensations Fernando Valenzuela or Dwight Gooden. It is not Cooperstown stalwarts Warren Spahn, Bob Gibson, Nolan Ryan, or Whitey Ford.

That one pitcher's name is John Stanley Sanford.

As the late New York Yankees sage Casey Stengel would say, you can look it up.

To make Jack's 70th birthday celebration truly special, son John planned to have a video of the historic seventh game of the 1962 World Series playing on a big screen throughout the party for all to see. After all, what are the odds that a kid who wasn't even considered the best pitcher on his high school team, a guy who was buried in the minor leagues for seven arduous years, a guy who had been discarded by one big league team and nearly placed on the expansion draft scrap heap by another, would end up starting the biggest baseball game of the season, Game Seven of the World Series?

Years after the 1962 World Series had ended, Jack was quoted as saying: "It was a two-million-to-one shot that it fell to me to pitch the seventh game of the Series. Not in my wildest boyhood dreams did I ever envision that a World Series would come along and I'd be the seventh game pitcher."

That game had been the pinnacle of Jack's pitching career, potentially his finest moment as a professional. As it turned out though, that game was also his most devastating moment, when San Francisco Giants slugger Willie McCovey lined out to end the game with a 1–0 gut-wrenching loss to the mighty New York Yankees, ending with it the Series, the season, and most of all, Jack's dream.

It had been a crushing blow—one that Jack took personally. But that had been 37 years—more than half of Jack's lifetime—ago. Plenty of time to heal. Plenty of time to get over the heartbreak, recover, and move on. Plenty of time, for most people, but not for Jack Sanford.

When the unsuspecting guest of honor walked into the great room of John Sanford's Palm City, Florida, home that afternoon, 80 celebrants screamed, "Surprise!" But all that Jack Sanford saw was the video of that dreaded Game Seven staring him in the face, forcing him to relive what, instead of being his finest hour, had turned out to be his worst nightmare.

Without saying a word, Jack, shocked and livid, whirled and marched back outside as stunned son John raced to catch up with him. By the time John reached his dad, Jack was seated in his car, seething, ready to drive away.

"What's wrong, Dad?" John asked frantically.

"I've played that game a thousand times in my dreams

and it always comes out the same," a somber Jack Sanford replied. "I'm sure as hell not going to watch it on TV."

To this day, the seventh game of the 1962 World Series is hailed as a baseball classic. But to Jack Sanford, one of the stars of the show, that game would forever be synonymous with heartbreak and failure. Nearly four decades later, he still could not bring himself to look.

On December 22, 1962, in the third panel of a nationally syndicated *Peanuts* comic strip by Charles M. Schulz—one of the best-known, most influential cartoonists of all time, and friend of Jack Sanford's—a glum Charlie Brown, the ultimate loser, was seen to suddenly bellow: "Why couldn't McCovey have hit the ball just three feet higher?"

A month later, the scene was repeated in a similar strip, only this time, Charlie Brown, still bemoaning the loss, screamed: "Or why couldn't McCovey have hit the ball even *two* feet higher?"

Why, indeed. Jack Sanford could not have said it any better himself. Three feet. Two feet. So close—and yet so far. It was the story of Jack's life.

Aaugh!

After several minutes in his car that May 1999 afternoon, Jack calmed down and John convinced his dad to return to the party—on the condition that John would turn off the TV and keep it off. No more World Series. No more Game Seven.

"Dad finally came back and everyone had a blast at the party," recalled John. "My mother, Patricia, said, after that crushing defeat in the seventh game of the '62 World Series, that Dad didn't speak to anyone for a month," added John. "He went to his grave tormented by that game."

"I dream about it every night," Jack told a reporter many years after Willie McCovey's wicked line drive became the heartbreaking final out in the World Series. "It never goes away."

In the hardscrabble 1930s and '40s, in the depressed, war-dominated, no-nonsense days before TV and Twitter, before selfies and smartphones, before iPods and Xboxes, every sandlot and every neighborhood park in America became a baseball field. And every young boy, whether remotely able or not, dreamed of someday playing baseball in the big leagues.

In the middle of the twentieth century, with professional football still in its infancy, and basketball and hockey barely blips on the country's consciousness, baseball, even in the darkest of days, was more than the undisputed Great American Pastime. It was a way out. An escape. An escape for fun-starved fans, whose humdrum daily lives were, more often than not, filled with drudgery if not despair. And an escape for those young men who were skilled enough or lucky enough to eke out a living playing the game that they had so loved as kids.

Growing up "on the wrong side of the tracks" in wealthy, suburban Wellesley, Massachusetts, some 15 miles west of Boston, where the big league Red Sox and Braves reigned supreme, little Johnny Sanford, as Jack was known in his youth, was no exception.

"I never called him Jack," recalled Sanford's eventual brother-in-law, Phil Reynolds, who was 11 when Jack began dating Phil's older sister, Patsy. "Some newspaper guy came up with that name when John was in the minors. John was known to pitch inside so maybe 'Jack' sounded more lethal."

Nephew Jim Sanford, 15 years younger than Jack, concurred. "To me, he was always 'Uncle John,'" Jim said. "Uncle John and my dad, Fred, were my heroes."

Five months after Jack was born on May 18, 1929, the U.S. stock market crashed, plunging Wellesley, Massachusetts, along with the rest of the country, into the Great Depression.

When Jack was a child, he contracted pneumonia. He was "so sickly, we were afraid we might lose him," Jack's mother recalled. Later, Jack underwent an appendectomy—on the family's kitchen table. "He was very proud of that," said daughter Laura. "And we still had that kitchen table in our house in Duxbury! My dad thought that was so funny."

Jack spurned his parents' efforts to interest him in music and instead followed his older brother, Fred, and sister Nancy onto the neighborhood baseball diamonds. Unlike the vast majority of young ballplayers pretending to be big leaguers on neighborhood sandlots across the country, blond, blue-eyed Jack Sanford eventually realized his dream.

Jack made it. But Jack Sanford never had it made. Certainly not in his own mind. While others, at least in the best of times, applauded and even revered him, Sanford, the major league baseball pitcher turned golf course manager, saw his own life as an uphill struggle nearly every step of the way. Jack was old school. He considered himself a hard worker, but never a great player—although to this day, nearly a half century after he hung up his glove, ardent baseball fans still remember his name.

Sanford never took shortcuts. Never did he take his craft for granted, or have a sense of entitlement about him. Never was he less than 100 percent committed to the task at hand.

In 1962, Jack became the first pitcher since ancient Hall of Famer Tim Keefe way back in 1888 to win 16 games in a row in a single season and also lead either league, National or American, in shutouts during any season (1960). The legendary Christy Mathewson never accomplished that. Neither did Walter Johnson, Cy Young, Bob Feller or any of game's other pitching icons.

But Jack Sanford did.

Admittedly, such statistics may be a bit obscure. They may be snickered at by snobbish students of the sabermetrics revolution. But they indisputably add up to quite a career—whether Jack Sanford was ever willing to admit it or not.

Jack signed with the Philadelphia Phillies in 1947 for a meager $125 a month after being rebuffed by the hometown Red Sox. Unlike most of the young men who toiled in the labyrinth that was then baseball's minor leagues, Jack eventually reached baseball's Big Show—but only after an arduous nine-year odyssey that included two years of military service.

Sanford signed with the Phillies the same year that Jackie Robinson broke baseball's color barrier with the Brooklyn Dodgers. By the time Sanford finally reached the big leagues for a cup of coffee with the Phillies in September 1956, Robinson's historic, game-changing career was coming to a premature end. On December 13, 1956, Robinson retired rather than accept a trade to the New York Giants. The Rookie of the Year Award that Sanford won in 1957 is now named after Robinson, who was its first recipient in 1947.

Few major leaguers, much less major league stars, have ever overcome so much, or waged such an uphill struggle to reach the highest levels of the game.

"Dad always told me, 'You weren't born rich so you better figure out what you love to do in life and make a job out of it,' " recalled son John. "His philosophy was you had to outwork everybody else in order to be successful. And if you love what you do, then it isn't really work. That was what led me to be a golf course architect."

Jack and son, John

"There was always a certain amount of anxiety no matter how well he was doing," said daughter Laura, Jack's oldest child. "He never gave himself the permission to feel good about himself, or the credit for his amazing accomplishments."

Added youngest daughter Susan, "I believe his life was one of struggle and perseverance."

"His whole life, he viewed himself as the underdog—all his rivals were bigger, stronger, faster, and smarter," John Sanford continued. "It was him alone against the rest of the world, not just in baseball but in every facet of life. I believe it was this philosophy that led to his success but also made for plenty of stress and strain."

When 1962 World Series standout Jack Sanford was finally featured in the popular, nationally circulated *Sport* magazine in March 1963, the story on him was entitled, "Jack Sanford's Grim World." And in those days, before *Sports Illustrated* outspent and overwhelmed the competition with its slick, photo-filled weekly approach, the monthly, fan-oriented *Sport* magazine was must-reading for the nation's sports aficionados.

Jack was voted the National League Rookie of the Year and named to the NL All-Star team in 1957 when he was 28 years old—well past the age when most ballplayers destined to ever amount to anything make their major league debuts. He won 19 games for the Philadelphia Phillies that summer and led the league strikeouts with 188 Ks.

In 1962, after Jack had been discarded by the Phillies, he won a near-record 16 games in a row for San Francisco as he pitched the Giants to their first pennant since they moved from New York to the West Coast in 1958. As the ace of that Giants pitching staff that also included Hall of Famer Juan Marichal and veterans Billy Pierce, Billy O'Dell, and Don Larsen of "Perfect Game" fame, Sanford started Games Two, Five, and Seven in the rain-delayed 1962 World Series against the New York Yankees.

In spite of the skepticism of others and his own self-doubt, Sanford enjoyed a major league career that spanned 12 seasons with the Phillies, Giants, California Angels, and Kansas City Athletics, and included 137 wins, 101 losses, and a 3.69 earned-run average. That's not Cooperstown caliber, certainly, but it's not chopped liver, either.

Jack pitched more than 200 innings in each of his first five seasons (1959-63) in San Francisco and topped the National League with 42 starts in 1963—at age 34.

Traded to the California Angels in 1965 and relegated to the bullpen, Jack won an American League-high 12 games in relief in 1966.

He was also an excellent hitter for a pitcher. In the '62 World Series, Jack delivered three hits in seven at-bats (.429), matching the production of New York Yankees icon Mickey Mantle, who managed just three hits in 25 trips to the plate (.120). Sanford also outhit his own Hall of Fame teammate Willie Mays .429 (3-for-7) to .250 (7-for-28) in the Series.

Three times he received votes for Most Valuable Player, twice in the National League and once in the American. Twice he finished among the Top 10.

In 1962, before separate Cy Young Awards were presented to the top pitchers in each league, Sanford finished second in the balloting for the best pitcher in baseball, behind the Los Angeles Dodgers' Don Drysdale, who won 25 games and led the league in strikeouts that summer.

In three different seasons, Jack finished among the Top 10 in the NL in victories. Twice, he was among the Top 10 in earned-run average, complete games, and strikeouts per nine innings pitched.

Not bad for a high-strung hurler who, as a five-foot-nine, 160-pound teenager, was told he was "too small" by Boston Red Sox scouts, snubbed by the Boston Braves, and labeled "no prospect" by his own high school coach.

Hall of Fame sportswriter Bob Stevens of the *San Francisco Examiner* may have best summed up Jack Sanford's career when he wrote: "Sanford didn't get a lot of credit because he wasn't a classic-looking pitcher. He was a bulky guy who would be a small-size right tackle on the football team. He wasn't delicate. He was out there to throw the baseball and he did it well. He wasn't afraid to brush back a hitter. He was an old-school pitcher. He wasn't a Cadillac but he was a damn good Buick."

Yet, despite all of his talent, all of his accomplishments, all of his undeniable success, Sanford remained a tortured and tormented soul.

"Thinking back on it, I got the feeling that Jack was very disappointed with his baseball career," said Jeff DeCiccio, a financial consultant from Massachusetts who became Jack's dear friend and who spent countless hours golfing, hunting, and fishing with him during his later years. "He failed when he lost the World Series to the Yankees. This tormented him for the rest of his years."

Whether spawned by his rough home life while growing up, terrified of his own abusive, alcoholic father, or his rejection as a young ballplayer fueled by seven years of frustration in the minor leagues, or a product of his personal insecurity, Jack's fiery temper and erratic mood impacted almost everyone who crossed his path.

Jack Sanford was often his own worst enemy—at home, on the baseball diamond, and later on the golf course. "He was extremely temperamental," recalled nephew Jim, who, despite the 15-year difference in their ages, spent countless hours with Jack before his professional baseball career began and again during Jack's 1957 rookie season in Philadelphia. "When things weren't going right, the way he thought things should go, he kind of flew off the handle. He never got mad at me. Never. He kind of hid it. But I could sense it."

During a minor league game in 1954, when his manager came out to the mound to take him out of the game, Jack refused to hand over the ball, earning himself a 10-day suspension.

The 1963 *Sport* magazine profile laid bare Jack's demeanor on and off the field. "Jack Sanford is a man of many moods, mostly bad," wrote well-respected sportswriter Bill Libby. "He is sullen and silent, turned inward, unwilling to give a thing away. When he doesn't turn his back on you and does talk, you sometimes wish he hadn't. He is cold and quick-tempered, given to profanities. But mostly, he is one hell of a pitcher."

In the Giants clubhouse, Sanford was known as "Smiling Jack," for the same reason, as Libby noted, that "some fat men are called 'Skinny' and some bald men are called 'Curly.'

"His blue eyes are hard and cold, shielded by heavy brows, and he squints around them," Libby wrote. "His hair is sandy, chopped short. His jaw is hinged, his face flexible, and he twists it into various expressions, most of them forbidding, defiant, scowling. He saves his smiles for his friends, and he doesn't make friends easily.

"Jack Sanford," Libby added, "takes victory just as he takes defeat—with a scowl."

In those days, except for the World Series, baseball

players and baseball teams were usually covered by a handful of local sportswriters and a couple of radio broadcasters, all of whom were beholden to the hometown team and thus tended to turn a blind eye to the players' shortcomings. Teams regularly paid for the hotel bills and travel expenses of the beat writers. Some teams even gave reporters the same daily meal money that they distributed to their players. No wonder writers were often accused of parroting the party line.

Imagine what life would be like for Jack, with his temper and his moods, in today's age of round-the-clock cable news, the ceaseless chatter of sports talk radio, and the unrelenting barrage of Twitter, Instagram, and smartphone camera shots. His conduct would constantly be under a microscope, in the spotlight, and in the headlines. Can you picture Jack's reaction after a game, especially a loss, if a fan ever asked him to lean in close to pose for a selfie?

Sanford's son, John, acknowledged that his dad was known for his explosive temper. "He always said that's what helped an average kid from Wellesley to make it in the bigs," John recalled. "He carried it over to the golf course, where it wasn't beneficial, but we didn't see much of it at home."

"As to my dad's so-called temper, he demanded so much from himself and was frustrated when he failed," added Laura. "Less than a perfect performance on his part was not sufficient; he was very competitive."

And maybe Jack Sanford had a right to feel a bit bitter. It is safe to say Sanford's career and accomplishments went largely unappreciated, both in Philadelphia and later in San Francisco, where he enjoyed his greatest success. According to Richard Johnson, the curator for the New England Sports Museum, which, by the way, does not feature any Sanford memorabilia, "He has been forgotten about, even by Giants fans, even though, for at least one season, he was the best pitcher on a very good pitching staff.

"Imagine," Johnson said, "how much a pitcher today with his skills, if developed properly, would be appreciated."

In today's game, a pitcher of Jack Sanford's stature, with Jack Sanford's statistics, might merit a salary of $8–10 million a year.

But Sanford excelled in the late 1950s and early '60s. According to Baseball-Reference.com, the most money he ever made playing baseball was $38,000 in 1964—the twilight of his career. That is less than 10 percent of today's major league minimum salary that is paid, not to stars or even journeymen, but only to the rawest of unproven, untested rookies.

According to the website PointAfter, Jack made a total of $123,000 in his 12-year major league career.

Bill Libby may have best summed up Sanford's career

in his 1963 *Sport* feature: "He's worked hard and waited long for everything he's ever gotten in baseball, and when success has come, disappointment has not been far behind."

In the 1962 World Series, the country finally saw what Jack's friends and family and baseball teammates already knew: that Jack Sanford was a tremendous competitor.

As Arnold Hano, one of the most prolific sportswriters of the period, a man who covered the San Francisco Giants throughout the '62 Series, wrote: "If I ever were to wander into an alley in the dark and I needed companions ... I'd have Jack Sanford with me. You can have Sonny Liston." Quite a tribute considering, at the time, Liston was the newly crowned heavyweight champion of the world and widely considered an indestructible brute.

With the odds seemingly stacked against him from the outset and at almost every turn, Jack Sanford went farther in his life and in his career than most men do. Much farther than he himself ever imagined possible. Still, he felt unfulfilled.

```
┌─────────────────────────────────────────────────────┐
│  BALL │1│  STRIKE │2│  OUT │1│                        │
│  FAIR-PLAY    1  2  3  4  5  6  7  8  9   TOTAL       │
│    by TRANSLUX                                        │
│  VISITOR □ □ □ □ □ □ □ □ □     □                      │
│  HOME    □ □ □ □ □ □ □ □ □     □                      │
│  ═══════════════════════════════════════════════     │
│         SCHOOL OF HARD KNOCKS                         │
└─────────────────────────────────────────────────────┘
```

John Stanley Sanford was born in Wellesley Hills, Massachusetts, a section of well-to-do Wellesley, on May 18, 1929, the youngest of four children in the working-class family of Frederick and Margaret Sanford.

Originally, Frederick Sanford's last name was Hatch. But his parents orphaned him at age five at the Boston Home for Little Wanderers because they felt they could no longer afford to feed him. When Frederick was about 12 years old he was adopted by an older, childless couple named Sanford, and Frederick took his adoptive father's last name. Jack's mother, Margaret Maloney, was an Irish immigrant who had been sent to America from County Mayo, Ireland, alone on a boat at age 12 to work as a domestic servant.

To this day, the Sanfords refer to their family home in Wellesley Hills as "Blightville."

Don't waste your time trying to look for "Blightville" on a map. It's a family thing, a name that is unique to the Sanfords. " 'Blightville' was a couple of homes on Oakland Circle in Wellesley Hills that were owned by my grandfather's adopted parents," explained Jack's nephew Jim, who, like Jack, grew up in Blightville. According to Jack's daughter Laura, Frederick's adoptive mother's maiden name was Annie Blight.

"We called it 'Blightville' because of the family name," Jim Sanford continued. "But that name also tied in with what everything looked like. The upkeep of the homes. We were in the slum section of Wellesley. We actually had outhouses.

"As a kid, I thought those houses were luxurious," Jim added. "But later, when I had a chance to go back and visit, I realized it really was a tough area.

"We lived at the bottom of a hill. I lived in the same house with my Uncle John and his family, my grandmother and grandfather, my great grandmother, my father, mother, and my brother. There were a lot of people in a very tiny house. My father had been in the navy and when he came home from the service [my parents] were waiting for a spot in one of the veterans' housing projects in Wellesley, so we moved in with

John's family and my grandfather and grandmother. Later, my grandfather actually sold the house right out from under my grandmother. She came home one day and the house was sold. Everybody had to move."

"All of my memories of Nana are positive, but she had a very tough life," John Sanford recalled of his grandmother.

"The town we grew up in was very affluent, most of us growing up there could not afford to move back," said Sanford's brother-in-law and long-time friend, Phil Reynolds. "John's family was from the other end of the economic scale."

When Jack was growing up, Frederick Sanford worked for the Wellesley Department of Public Works. Later, he took a job as an engineer in a wool-processing plant in nearby Newton. Once Jack and his siblings started school, their mother, Margaret, sometimes worked outside the home to help make ends meet. Jack was quite close to her and to his siblings Nancy and Fred, as Phil Reynolds recalled.

When the wife of Jack's older brother, Fred Jr., passed away in 1957, leaving six children, Jack's mother, then in her mid-60s, stepped in to help Fred raise the youngsters. For that, local radio station WKOX presented Margaret Sanford with a "Mother of the Year" award.

Later in life, after Jack retired from baseball, golf

would become his passion. But he was first exposed to the game as a toddler. "When John was only two and a half, his father got him a golf ball and a toy club," Margaret Sanford recalled years ago. "He'd go outside and hit that ball around by the hour. Then the ball got lost. We had no peace until his father got another one."

Jack's parents attempted to interest him in music. They signed him up for piano lessons, but after 12 or 13 sessions, his mother said, "his teacher told us we were just wasting our money." Sanford also took violin lessons for a while. The teacher promised to give him the instrument if he completed 20 lessons. After 19 lessons, Jack quit.

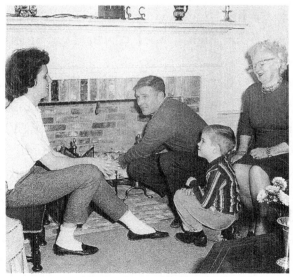

Pat, Jack, John, and Margaret

With an older brother and sister who liked to play baseball, it was inevitable that young Jack would catch the baseball bug. He couldn't get enough of the game, constantly pestering the older boys in the neighborhood to let him join them on the diamond. Jack's older sister Nancy was a good athlete and the 13- and 14-year-olds in the neighborhood always wanted her on their teams. And Nancy would tell them, "I won't play unless you let John play, too."

Jack played some football in high school, even though his older brother, Fred, once a promising baseball pitcher himself, had injured his shoulder playing football. But baseball was always where Jack's heart was. "If he'd had the same desire in football that he did in baseball, he'd have made a fine single-wing halfback or a T-formation quarterback," his high school coach, Ted Steeves, later declared.

Jack didn't play basketball or hockey. He would have, but he had to spend the winter months catching up on his schoolwork. He attended Wellesley High School, also known as Gamaliel Bradford High School. Wellesley was and is known for one of the best public school systems in Massachusetts, turning out the likes of Sylvia Plath and Anne Sexton. But Jack's schoolteachers remembered him as a sullen, rebellious boy with lousy grades. "Most of the time I wasn't available for sports in that second semester," Sanford admitted. "Usually, my marks were a little low."

"We used to keep after him about his marks," his mother recalled. "But it didn't seem to do much good. He just wasn't interested."

Jack's High School Yearbook Picture

Although Wellesley boasts one of the highest percentages of residents with advanced degrees in the country, Jack attended only one semester at Bentley University. He was too busy playing baseball. Throughout his life, whenever anyone asked where he went to college, Jack would reply, "The school of hard knocks."

Sanford was a good pitcher in high school but there were few pro scouts lurking in the stands, taking notes during his games. "He really came to life as a senior," said 1946 Wellesley High grad Jim Decker. In Jack's final game at Wellesley High, on June 6, 1947, he pitched a no-hitter against Needham High.

"My sister Patsy told me all about it and said she was dating this guy," recalled Phil Reynolds. "Soon after that, he appeared and even though I was only eleven, we got along pretty well. I loved sports so we had something in common. Unfortunately for me, I did not have the talent.

"My sister and John probably loved it when I tagged along on their dates to the movies. Their romance was not lavish, as John came from very meager means. My mother was not happy because he was of Irish descent, Catholic, poor, and he did not like to wear a necktie to Sunday dinner."

Early in the summer of 1947, shortly after Jack graduated from high school, his sister Nancy, who played third base on a sandlot softball team and who had gotten him into so many games with the older boys over the years, prodded him to go to a Red Sox tryout camp at Fenway Park in Boston. "My aunt Nancy made sure uncle John went to all his practices and all his high school games," said Jim Sanford. "She was a committed older sister." Afraid that Jack, who always lacked for self-confidence, would chicken out, Nancy packed his spikes and glove along with a couple of sandwiches in a shopping bag and personally put him on the trolley that ran by Fenway Park.

"There were a couple of hundred boys there," Jack later recalled. "They told me to take the mound. When I was through, they called me over and said they thought I was too small. They said something about coming back next year when I got more growth." Bear in mind, in the 1940s, the height of the average American male was five foot seven and a half. "I was real disappointed and I went over and sat down," Jack continued. "There was a fellow sitting there and he asked my name and address."

That stranger was a "bird dog" named Frank Seyboth, who was paid to scour the bushes, searching for undiscovered talent for 50-year-old Phillies area scout Joe LaBate, who had earned a reputation as a talent sleuth years earlier on behalf of the Brooklyn Dodgers. "I told him where he could reach me," Sanford continued, "but I didn't hear anything from him for a couple of months."

As fate would have it, Wellesley, Massachusetts, also happened to be home to construction tycoon Lou Perini, who had purchased the major league Boston Braves in 1945, when Jack Sanford was a sophomore at Wellesley High. Perini Corporation, which was founded in 1894 by Lou Perini's grandfather, Bonfiglio Perini, was one of the world's largest privately owned construction companies, involved in building bridges, highways, dams, airports, and projects like the Alaska pipeline.

"John's best friend was Lou Perini Jr., the son of the owner of the Boston Braves and at the upper echelon, wealth-wise. John, of course, was at the bottom," recalled Phil Reynolds. Sanford had met Lou Jr. in a catechism class and the two youngsters formed a lifelong friendship. This connection was to become very important after Jack retired from baseball.

In addition, Sanford's high school baseball coach, Harold Goodnough, was a part-time scout for the Braves. It would have seemed only natural if Sanford had signed a contract to play baseball for the Braves.

What's more, as soon as Jack was old enough to drive, the elder Perini gave him a part-time job chauffeuring him around Boston in his limousine. "Dad had tremendous respect for Lou Sr. and looked up to him as a father figure," recalled John Sanford. "It always bothered him that he was so close to the owner of the Boston Braves but was never asked to try out for the team."

According to Jack himself, Perini did offer him a professional contract when he was finishing high school. "But he had never seen me pitch and I had the feeling he was just trying to do me a favor," Sanford told sportswriter Harry T. Paxton in a 1958 interview for the *Saturday Evening Post*, a national publication of major import in the 1950s. "I wanted to get started on my own."

"Mr. Perini tried hard to talk John out of going into professional baseball, knowing the failure rate was very high and the lower minor leagues pretty grungy," said Phil Reynolds.

Some suspected Goodnough may have sabotaged Jack's chances of signing with the Braves. The elder Perini all but confirmed that in his interview with Paxton for the 1958 article. "Apparently Hal Goodnough did not consider at the time that Jack Sanford had major league potential and did not recommend to the Braves that he be signed for the club," Perini said.

Eventually, Sanford, who had spent the summer of '47 unsuccessfully trying out for independent teams in Burlington, Vermont, and in Canada, did hear back from Seyboth. "I got a letter saying to meet him at the Hotel Kenmore in Boston if I wanted to sign with the Phillies' farm system," recalled Jack, by then 19 and eager to get on with his life.

Baseball did not have an amateur draft in those days. Teams depended on networks of scouts and occasional tryout camps to find and sign young talent. Each player was on his own—at the mercy of whatever team or teams might be willing to offer him a job. There was little negotiation or bargaining, especially for players like Jack, who weren't highly scouted or considered blue chip.

"Take it or leave it," Seyboth demanded, pushing a contract calling for a paltry salary of $125 a month across the table.

Jack took it. Meager as that contract may sound by today's inflated standards, it was not so far out of line at the time. For example, Billy Martin, who would later gain fame and notoriety as the second baseman and subsequently the manager of the New York Yankees and several other teams, signed his first minor league contract in 1946 for $200 a month.

~

Jack was 23, still toiling in the minor leagues and living at home with his mother during the offseason when, in 1952, his father, Frederick, passed away.

"My grandfather was a big drinker," recalled Jim Sanford, who grew up in the same house with Jack and Frederick. "He caused a lot of problems. And he wasn't too good to my uncle John or to my father until my father and my uncle got old enough to physically handle themselves. Then they put my grandfather in his place.

"My father came home one night and found my grandfather slapping my grandmother around. He told him, 'That's never going to happen again.' And my father kicked my grandfather out of the house. My grandfather passed away not too long after that."

As Jack's daughter Laura recounted, "My grandfather ('Grampa' per cousin Jimmy) was headed out to where he worked at the aqueducts at the Quabbin Reservoir for the MDC (Metropolitan District Commission) in a snowstorm. His truck got stuck in the snow on the side of the road on Belmont Hill in Worcester. Apparently, Grampa had some whiskey in his truck or went to the liquor store on foot and got some and went back to his truck to drink it. He got plowed in and his truck was completely covered with snow. When the snow melted three days later, the truck was out of gas, the key was in the ignition, and the ignition was 'on.' It was determined that Grampa died of carbon monoxide poisoning due to being plowed in, his exhaust pipe blocked by the snow. He must have fallen asleep with the truck running. The insurance company claimed that Grampa's death was intentional, but my grandmother prevailed to prove that his death was accidental."

"As a result, John did not drink in those early years; he did not want to be like his old man," recalled Phil Reynolds. "With or without a necktie John often ate dinner with us on Sunday. Even though my mother might have a drink, John did not partake. We used to go to Ken's Steakhouse in Framingham in a large group. I never recall John having a drink. [He] did have the habit of ordering well-done steaks and then drowning them in ketchup. Some ten years later he still ate his steaks the same way," Reynolds added. According to Patricia Sanford, Laura said, Jack did not begin drinking alcohol until he was about 27.

"I never met my grandfather; he died before I was born, and Dad didn't talk about him much, but when he did it was always negative," said son John Sanford. "He said his dad was a raging alcoholic who would beat the crap out of whoever was in the way when he got home from work. Dad told stories of being so scared of him when he was a kid that he would piss his pants when he heard the 'old man' coming in the door."

After Frederick passed away, Jack bought a house for himself and his mother in Weston, Massachusetts, where he lived until he married Patricia in 1955.

"Sometimes, he'd just sit there for an hour or more, not saying a word," Margaret Sanford recalled of her son Jack in an interview for the *Saturday Evening Post* article. "Finally, I'd say, 'What in the world are you thinking about?' He'd say, 'Oh, I was just thinking about how I could have won that game last August if I'd done something different.'

"At night, I'd hear him shouting in his sleep, 'Get back!' and 'I'll take it!'

"There was one year when his father was still living when we had young Fred and his family and my mother-in-law all staying with us," Margaret continued. "When John came home for the winter we gave him the bedroom next to my mother-in-law. He almost scared her to death. He'd be waving his arms around, banging the partition, playing baseball in his sleep. By the time the winter was over, he'd actually worn a hole in that partition."

"On many occasions, when visiting Jack in West Palm Beach [Florida], he would wake us up in the middle of the night—hollering and banging on the wall," Jack's friend Jeff DeCiccio recalled. "In the morning, pictures were crooked on the walls.

"Many years later, we asked him about those wake-up nights," DeCiccio continued. "He told us, 'I was back at Yankee Stadium.'

" 'Do you really want to hear about this?' Jack would ask. Jack could be very moody. He could hold a grudge. He was very private. Telling us about that day in Yankee Stadium was like he was telling us something shameful about his life. He said, 'Jeffrey, you have no idea what it was like. One hundred thousand people, all yelling your name: San-ford! San-ford! San-ford!' "

Jack Sanford had, indeed, come a long way from Blightville.

BALL	0	STRIKE	2	OUT	2

FAIR-PLAY by TRANSLUX	1	2	3	4	5	6	7	8	9	TOTAL
VISITOR										
HOME										

I HAD TO CREEP UP THE HARD WAY

In 1947, the Philadelphia Phillies, anxious to build up their arsenal of talented young pitchers—a costly effort that would produce the "Whiz Kids" and lead to the National League pennant in 1950—threw a $65,000 bonus at lefty Curt Simmons, who, coincidentally, was one day younger than Jack Sanford. The following year, the Phillies bestowed a $25,000 bonus on another pitcher, future Hall of Famer Robin Roberts.

However, when it came time to sign hard-throwing young Jack Sanford in 1947, all that those same Phillies offered was a Class D contract for 1948 worth a paltry $750 a year—no bonus—plus a train ticket, coach of course, to Bradford, Pennsylvania, where the Phils fielded a team in the lowly Pennsylvania-Ontario-New York League, also known as the Pony League. Class D was the bottom rung in their farm system, basically the equivalent of low Class A today.

Bradford was also where future Hall of Fame pitcher Warren Spahn, who would go on to become the poster boy for late bloomers, had made his professional debut in 1940.

When Sanford signed, little did he or anyone else realize that, unlike bonus babies Simmons and Roberts, it would be nine long years before Jack would set foot in the big leagues. And by then his minor league ledger would read like a Rand McNally road map.

But World War II had been over for two years and, like the rest of the country, Jack was looking to the future. Having just spent a frustrating first summer out of high school without a job, and failing to make the independent teams in Burlington and Canada, Jack was desperate enough to grab the Phillies' offer and opportunity, meager though it may have been even by 1947 standards. It almost turned out to be the last baseball contract Jack Sanford ever signed.

The 1948 Bradford Blue Wings were the worst team in the Pony League, and Sanford, wild and ineffective with a 1–6 record and a 7.06 earned-run average, was the worst pitcher on that woeful team.

After 13 games, Jack was demoted to Dover,

Delaware, another Phillies Class D outpost, in the Eastern Shore League. At Dover, Jack fared even worse, losing nine games while winning just two and compiling a 7.28 ERA. To earn a little extra money and maybe to try to make himself more useful, Jack volunteered to drive the team bus. Even with Sanford behind the steering wheel on road trips—surely not because of it—the 1948 Dover Phillies were the worst team in all of organized baseball that summer, mustering a pitiful 26–100 record.

Other than Jack, only one other player on the '48 Dover Phillies, shortstop Mickey Micelotta, would ever see the light of day in the major leagues. Micelotta appeared in 17 games with the Phillies in 1954–55, while Jack was still toiling in the minors, but Micelotta never collected a big league hit. In 1949, the entire Eastern Shore League went out of business.

Meanwhile, back in Boston, the Braves, owned by Jack's former employer and father figure Lou Perini, were winning the 1948 National League pennant.

In Philadelphia, some disgusted members of the Phillies front office wanted to release the entire Dover roster and start over from scratch. In those days, low-level minor league baseball players were a dime a dozen. In 1950, there would be 430 mostly long-forgotten minor league teams, competing in 57 different leagues around the country.

Near the end of the 1948 season, veteran Phillies scout Jocko Collins was dispatched to Dover to determine whether any of the players on the Class D team were worth salvaging. Collins ended up recommending that the organization hang on to Sanford and a few others, at least for one more season. "Sanford's fastball was alive," Collins later recalled. "He threw extra hard. And I was always told, if a fellow threw a live ball, no matter how wild he was, he was major league material."

At the moment, however, the bright lights of the big leagues seemed hopelessly far away.

The Phillies sent Sanford back to Class D in 1949, this time to Americus, Georgia, in the Georgia-Florida League. Thanks to some timely pointers from Phillies minor league pitching instructor George Earnshaw, who had won 46 games for the 1929–30 world champion Philadelphia Athletics, Sanford showed marked improvement, winning 15 games while losing nine with a 4.39 ERA in 1949, despite battling a sore arm for much of the summer.

Jack jumped to Class B Wilmington, Delaware, a suburb of Philadelphia, in 1950 and proved himself worthy of the promotion by posting a 12–4 record with a 3.71 ERA for the Blue Rocks in the Interstate League.

In 1951, the reigning National League champion Phillies sent Sanford, by now a bona fide big league prospect, to Class A Schenectady in the Eastern League. There, Jack was 15–11 in '51 and 16–8 in '52, when, for the first time, he yielded less than three earned runs (2.94) per game. In both seasons he was the winningest pitcher on the Blue Jays team.

In 1952, Sanford was finally invited to spring training with the Phillies in Clearwater, Florida, for the first time. In Jack's mind, he was ready for the big leagues. And he let his bosses know it.

"About his fourth year in the organization, he had a row with [farm system director] Joe Reardon," recalled former Phillies assistant farm director Eddie Collins Jr. "Jack thought he wasn't getting ahead fast enough. There were hard feelings.

"But with all this talk about Jack's temperament, it should be understood that he was never a bad fellow to have on a ballclub. There are some fellows who are pretty good ballplayers, but such a bad influence that you hate to have them around. Jack was never like that. He was no troublemaker in the clubhouse and he always gave you his best on the field."

Today, Clearwater is a booming vacation destination. But when Jack Sanford first arrived in 1952, it was still a sleepy, hard-to-get-to, largely segregated Southern beach town of about 20,000 people. The Phillies played their spring exhibition games in a dilapidated ballpark known as Athletic Field, which had previously been used by the

Brooklyn Dodgers and Cleveland Indians, dating back to 1923. The field was surrounded by a wooden fence and a wire screen. The wooden stands seated fewer than 3,000 fans. According to Phillies catcher Andy Seminick, "The field was nothing but sand and seashells. It was brutal." As Philadelphia sportswriter Stan Baumgartner put it, "The outfield is a bucket of sand." The infield was so rocky the players referred to it as "Iwo Jima."

In 1955, while Jack was in the service, the Phillies moved into the new Jack Russell Stadium nearby. However, they continued to hold their daily practice sessions at Athletic Field.

Today's millionaire ballplayers rent mansions on the Gulf or on a golf course during spring training. But in Jack's years with the Phillies, players stayed two to a room at the team hotel and walked to and from practice each day. Despite the Florida heat and humidity, air conditioning was not available in all of the rooms at that hotel until 1955.

Each spring, Sanford would be the hardest thrower in the Phillies camp. And, at the end of training camp each year, he would be sent back down to the minor leagues. Naturally, he grew more and more frustrated. One year, informed again of his demotion, Jack reportedly threatened to punch a Phillies front office executive. Another spring, he argued with traveling secretary Johnny Wise when Wise handed Jack his train ticket back to the boondocks.

"Why was I sent down?" Jack angrily demanded to know, even though Wise was certainly not the one who had made that decision. "Did I have a curveball? Did I have a fastball?"

"You did, indeed, have those things," Wise replied, keeping his cool. "You also have the reddest ass in baseball."

In those days, before free agency and arbitration, ballplayers—especially lowly minor leaguers—did not talk back to club officials. Ballplayers, particularly minor leaguers, were considered chattel and expendable. But Sanford refused to accept the perception that he was merely a wild, mediocre minor league pitcher.

Each spring, he would ride the train from Massachusetts through Philadelphia on his way to training camp in Florida. "I can remember looking out the train window at Shibe Park [where the Phillies played] when I went through the North Philadelphia station every year," Jack recalled. "I might have been going to East Oshkosh, but I'd tell myself, 'That's where you'll be pitching one of these days.'"

As Bill Libby wrote in his March 1963 profile of Sanford, "He's been around, and he's been kicked around, usually back to the minors."

From 1949 through 1954, Jack won a combined 80 games in the minors while losing 59. In four of those six seasons he topped 200 innings pitched. Impressive numbers. But in four of those six years, he also walked more than 100 batters. As a result, until 1957, Jack never saw the City of Brotherly Love, except through the window of the train.

~

Like most ballplayers, both in the major leagues and most certainly in the minors, Sanford took offseason jobs to help make ends meet. One winter during his minor league days, Jack went back to work as a chauffeur for Lou Perini. Another year, he worked as a salesman for the Regal Corrugated Box Company.

"At the end of his first two seasons in the low minors, John would return to Wellesley and drive the delivery truck for the Wellesley Hills Market," recalled Phil Reynolds. "Sometimes I would drive around with him. I remember that he made thirty-five dollars a week delivering groceries, plus an occasional tip. So there was not a bunch of money. We always had dogs at home and if I couldn't ride in the delivery truck with him, he often took the dog."

During the baseball offseasons in the early 1950s, when young Jack wasn't working, he spent time with his girlfriend and wife-to-be, Patricia Reynolds, or went hunting, often alone. "That was about all I did," Sanford said. "I didn't have many friends in Wellesley. I wasn't a good mixer is the way, I guess, you'd put it."

Sometimes, Patricia's younger brother, Phil, would go hunting with Jack. "Really, it was him hunting and me being the gofer, running around a wooded area to see if I could scare up some birds for him," Phil Reynolds recalled.

"Another spot where we would go was the town dump where John would shoot rats until he ran out of ammo or I was so cold he would take me home. Some of the funniest times were when we went coon hunting. Once Patsy decided she wanted to go to see what we were up to out in the middle of the night. I remember her tripping over something and falling flat into the damp ground more than once. She didn't ask to go after that."

Jack's other hunting buddy was his nephew Jim. "When I was five or six years old, Uncle John used to take me out hunting with his .22 in the woods across the street from where we lived," Jim Sanford recalled. "We'd go shoot rabbits. He taught me how to fire a gun. When Uncle John was around, everything happened, you know. It was exciting. Very exciting."

~

In 1953, playing with Baltimore, then in its final season in the Triple-A International League, Sanford was surrounded by future major leaguers and posted a 14–13 record.

"When John began to climb the ladder playing baseball, it was amazing that we could get his games on the radio, sometimes very weakly, but nonetheless it was something," recalled Phil Reynolds. "At least we were able to follow him. In 1953, his older brother, Fred, and I would drive out to Springfield, Massachusetts, to see him pitch against the local team. But I actually saw John pitch very few times. Just as he got called up to the majors, I went into the service. It would be 1958 before I saw him in a live game in the major leagues."

In 1954 Jack again failed to stick with the Phillies and he was sent back to AAA, this time to Syracuse. "I had to creep up the hard way," Sanford once said. "They say, if you can't make the majors in five years you'd better quit. I almost did."

In August of 1954, Sanford's frustration boiled over when Syracuse Chiefs manager Skeeter Newsome came out to the mound to take Jack out of a game in Havana, Cuba. "I wouldn't leave the mound," Sanford recounted years later in the *Saturday Evening Post*. "Skeeter reached for the ball and I kind of pulled away and knocked the ball out behind second base. It made Skeeter look bad. Shucks, I wasn't thinking. I was totally wrong. I got suspended for ten days."

Nevertheless, despite the incident in Havana, and Sanford's disappointing 8–14 record in 1954, Roy Hamey, the Phillies' new general manager, informed reporters that Jack figured prominently in the team's pitching plans for '55. Unfortunately for Jack, he also figured in the U.S. Army's plans. He was drafted in October 1954, further delaying his prolonged quest to reach the big leagues.

Unlike some young players, in Jack's case the long wait certainly wasn't because of a lack of desire or determination. In fact, Sanford's progress may have been hindered by his own unbridled intensity, which, at times, caused him to lose control—of his temper and of his bread-and-butter fastball. As Eddie Collins Jr. recalled in the 1958 *Saturday Evening Post* article, "When Jack had a two-and-two count on a batter, and then the umpire gave him what he thought was a bad call, he'd blow his top. It would unsettle him so much that he couldn't do what he wanted to with the next pitch. It's generally agreed that to get good stuff on the ball, a pitcher has to be a little relaxed. He can't be too tense and tightened up."

"He was a real red-ass," recalled Johnny Wise. "When an umpire called one against him, he'd stomp around the infield the next couple of minutes the way Russ Meyer [a temperamental Phillies pitcher known as 'The Mad Monk' and 'Rowdy Russ'] used to."

Sanford himself acknowledged that his temper was often a problem. "I guess maybe it was insecurity more than anything else," Jack admitted in 1958. "I didn't have anything outside of baseball."

Even as a youngster, Sanford could be difficult to deal with. Ted Steeves was the head football coach and assistant baseball coach at Wellesley High School during Sanford's years there. In 1958, Steeves was asked by sportswriter Harry T. Paxton for a few comments regarding Jack. Steeves, by then the athletic director, responded, "Is this on or off the record?" That right there was a hint as to how Steeves had felt about young Sanford.

Told that the interview was, indeed, on the record, Steeves, no doubt choosing his words carefully, replied, "John was a boy with a chip-on-the-shoulder attitude. He was quick to take offense. He resisted instruction and correction. He didn't like to conform to regulations. Hal

Goodnough, the baseball coach, really had to struggle with him." One shudders to think what Steeves might have said if he had been assured his remarks were off the record.

However, like most basically good kids, young John Sanford, the rebel, eventually grew up. "Last October, John came back to Wellesley for a testimonial dinner, and I was amazed at what a nice guy he'd become," Steeves declared in 1958. "He handled himself perfectly. He deserves all the more credit because he started out the other way."

As Bud Hines, a gym instructor and trainer at Wellesley High recalled in an interview for the same *Saturday Evening Post* article, "This was a boy who, when he was in school here, would just as soon tell an instructor to go chase himself as he would another kid.

"After he got started in baseball, he'd sometimes come over during the offseason and work out playing basketball. One day he sprained his ankle. I gave him some whirlpool bath treatments and he left on schedule for spring training. Well, he no sooner got down to Florida that spring than he sent the Mrs. and myself a basket of preserves with a card saying, 'In appreciation of all you've done for me.'

"What a change from the old days," Hines declared. "Why, all I'd done was put him in the whirlpool a couple of times."

Sanford's two-year stint in the army cost him

precious time on the pitcher's mound, but it may also have been the turning point in his often troubled career. In 1958, after he had finally reached the big leagues where he found almost instant stardom, Sanford was asked by Harry Paxton if his 10-day suspension with Syracuse in 1954 had been what convinced him he had to get his temper under control. "No, I don't think it was," responded Sanford. "I don't think I reached the turning point until I was in the service."

Jack married Patricia on January 2, 1955, while he was on a furlough in the army. Their daughter Laura was born 10 months later, while he was stationed at Fort Bliss in El Paso, Texas.

Laura, Jack, and Pat

While in the army, Sanford trained as a missile technician at the Nike base. But he spent most of his time pitching for the Fort Bliss baseball team, hurling five no-hitters. "Unofficially, I had the running of the ballclub at Fort Bliss, although officially there was an officer that ran it," Jack recalled. "A lot of times I had to take a pitcher out of the ballgame and I learned how it was for a manager. I knew how bad the pitcher felt and it was agony to take him out, but it had to be done. We were trying to win."

Sanford's pitching prowess in the army probably kept him out of the Korean War, according to his son, John. "There was a general who wanted him for the army team," the younger Sanford said.

Joe Morgan, who would later play in the major leagues for four years and manage the Boston Red Sox from 1988 through 1991, had played against Sanford when the two were in high school but was not particularly impressed. So when Morgan's army team from Oklahoma engaged Sanford's Fort Bliss team in a tournament, Morgan advised his teammates not to worry. "I told our guys that we wouldn't have any problem with Sanford when I heard he was pitching," Morgan recalled years later. "He shut us out, 5–0, on two hits," Morgan admitted. "He got a lot better."

Sanford himself believed he grew stronger in his arms and shoulders during his two years in the army. By then he was almost six feet tall and weighed nearly 200 pounds. Jack was convinced he was ready to pitch in the big leagues. Of course, he had felt that way for years. The next mountain he would have to climb would be proving it.

```
┌─────────────────────────────────────────────────────┐
│   BALL☐    STRIKE☐    OUT☐                           │
├─────────────────────────────────────────────────────┤
│ FAIR-PLAY    1  2  3  4  5  6  7  8  9   TOTAL       │
│ by TRANSLUX                                           │
│ VISITOR  ☐ ☐ ☐ ☐ ☐ ☐ ☐ ☐ ☐    ☐                     │
│ HOME     ☐ ☐ ☐ ☐ ☐ ☐ ☐ ☐ ☐    ☐                     │
├─────────────────────────────────────────────────────┤
│ ONE GOOD YEAR DOESN'T CONVINCE ME                    │
└─────────────────────────────────────────────────────┘
```

In 1957, Dwight Eisenhower was in the White House. Richard Nixon was his vice president. The Soviet Union had launched Sputnik. A first-class postage stamp cost three cents. And, at the advanced age, at least by baseball standards, of 28, after having been buried in the bush leagues since 1948, hard-throwing Jack Sanford suddenly burst onto the big league scene, winning 19 games while losing only eight for the otherwise forlorn fifth-place Philadelphia Phillies.

The previously unheralded, virtually unheard-of Sanford also led the National League in strikeouts with 188 during his sensational summer of '57. Quite an accomplishment for a pitcher who had for so long struggled in the minor leagues with his command and his control.

JACK SANDFORD, Phillies

Of Jack's 19 wins that season, 15 were complete games—a remarkable statistic that would be almost unimaginable in baseball today. What's more, in 13 of those complete games, Jack held opponents to two runs or less—hence his career-best 3.08 earned-run average.

It truly was an epic season, especially in light of Jack's laborious past. And all of this was accomplished with a team that finished in fifth place in the eight-team National League, 38 games behind the pennant-winning Milwaukee Braves—owned by Sanford's friend and former employer Lou Perini, who had moved the franchise from Boston in 1953.

All in all, it was enough to make critics and even ardent fans wonder why the Phillies had waited so long to bring Jack Sanford to the big leagues. In fact, in September of 1956, when the Phillies finally decided to summon Sanford to venerable Connie Mack Stadium (Shibe Park had been renamed in 1953), it initially was merely to throw batting practice to the big leaguers for a few days while Jack, who had not pitched professionally for two years, was on a 30-day pre-discharge furlough from the army.

However, Phillies pitching coach Whitlow Wyatt, who had begun pitching in the big leagues for the Detroit Tigers in 1929, the year Jack was born, and who had won 106 games during his 16-year career, noticed Sanford's blazing fastball during BP and suggested to manager Mayo Smith—who had himself toiled for 18 years in the minor leagues as a player—that they throw their temporary new pitcher into a real game.

After all, what did Smith and the Phillies have to lose? They were stuck in fifth place, 20 games out of first, going nowhere fast. So, on September 16, after the Phillies had dropped the opener of a Sunday doubleheader against the Chicago Cubs, Smith sent his unknown, unproved right-hander out to the mound to start the second game before a meager gathering of 7,408 fans.

And, although it was belated, at least in Jack's mind, he certainly made quite a debut. Jack lasted seven innings in his first-ever appearance in a major league uniform on a major league mound, before a blister on his finger popped, forcing him to leave the game. He allowed just four hits and one run, although he did walk eight, to at long last earn his first major league victory at 27 years of age.

"Where has that fellow been all this time?" Mayo Smith wondered aloud. "I can't see how a fellow who can pitch that well spent seven years in the minor leagues."

Neither could Jack.

"Why in the world hasn't a fellow who can throw like that had an opportunity to pitch up here before?" chimed in Whit Wyatt.

"You can bet he'll be with us next year," Smith promised.

Following his victory, Sanford appeared in two more games in relief in September 1956, allowing one run on three hits in six innings of work out of the bullpen to finish the season with a 1.38 ERA. However, Jack's three scoreless innings of one-hit relief against the world champion Brooklyn Dodgers on September 25 went largely overlooked because the Dodgers' Sal Maglie threw a no-hitter against the Phillies that afternoon. Nevertheless, Jack told everyone who would listen, "I know I can pitch up here."

Sanford had always had small hands and short fingers which made it difficult to get a good grip on the ball. When he joined the Phillies that September, he noticed that the middle finger on his pitching hand tended to go numb after two or three innings. That apparently was the result of an arm injury suffered during a scuffle while he was in the service. "I got into a scrap in a ballgame," Jack explained at the time.

But there was more to the story than that. "My dad once told me a story about a friend of his by the name of Joe Calderon, whom he played baseball with in the army," recalled Jack's middle daughter, Nancy, who was born in 1961. "While playing on the army team at Fort Bliss, he and Joe became close friends. During a game in Sinton, Texas, a player on the opposing team started shouting racial slurs at Joe, who was Hispanic. When this player got up to bat, my dad was so mad and upset he threw a fastball at him and hit him hard. The batter rushed my dad and the fight was on. My dad injured his shoulder or his arm and he never fully recovered.

"Several years ago, after my dad had passed away, a friend of mine who knew Joe Calderon introduced us," Nancy continued. "I met Joe a couple of times and we talked about my dad and army baseball. Joe showed me scrapbooks of their army baseball days and told me this same story about the fight. Joe truly respected and admired my dad and I know the feelings were mutual."

After the 1957 season ended, the Phillies sent Sanford for treatment. The first doctor Jack saw wanted to operate. Jack sought a second opinion and that physician prescribed medication instead. But even with the pills, Sanford's fingertips would still go numb in cold weather and he often used a hand warmer on the bench during games. It troubled him throughout his big league career and prompted him to use a lot of rosin.

Always a hard thrower, Sanford found his greatest success after pitching coach Whit Wyatt worked with him during the Phillies' 1957 three-week pre–spring training "rookie school" in Florida to remake his slow, sweeping curve into a sharp downward hook that could keep hitters off-balance and stop them from simply sitting on his fastball. Such pre–spring training sessions, where teams could fine-tune the talents of young prospects away from the prying eyes of the public and the press, were commonplace in those days.

"Wyatt changed the position of my thumb and had me roll my wrist more," Jack explained. "Now I consistently put the ball where I want it."

"If this kid can't win in the big leagues, nobody can," Mayo Smith told confidants.

"I've got to make it," Sanford vowed during spring training. "I'm married now and we have a little girl. I've got to get that big league money. I'm up here now and I'm not going to blow it. I can't do much of anything except throw a baseball. And I certainly don't want to go back to driving a bus at my age."

Today, Jack Sanford and former Phillies manager Mayo Smith are both enshrined in the Palm Beach

County Sports Hall of Fame in Florida.

Despite Jack's victory near the end of the '56 season and Smith's comments at the start of the 1957 season, Sanford continued to underestimate his own ability. Jack suspected the Phillies only kept him on the squad because, as a returning serviceman, he didn't count against their 25-man roster limit and therefore gave them the advantage of an "extra" player.

Jack's lack of self-confidence was understandable. By 1957, Robin Roberts, who had signed with the Phillies at about the same time Sanford did, had 179 big league victories under his belt and was considered the ace of the Phils' pitching staff. Curt Simmons, who also signed in 1948, had 96 career wins. Meanwhile, Jack Sanford had a not-so-grand total of one major league win next to his name.

The Phillies' 1957 pitching staff was divided between veterans Roberts, Simmons, and Harvey Haddix, and a hard-drinking band of youngsters who had been christened "The Dalton Gang" by Philadelphia sportswriters who likened Dick "Turk" Farrell, Jack Meyer, Seth Morehead, and Jim "Bear" Owens to a gang of Wild West outlaws. Mayo Smith, a laissez-faire manager who believed in leaving his players alone and letting them play, had clearly lost control.

Former teammate Chuck Essegian included Jack in that group. "We had some characters, Dick Farrell, Seth

Morehead, Jim Owens, and Jack Sanford," Essegian said without elaborating. Against that distracting, potentially disruptive backdrop, Sanford, one of seven rookies on the Phillies team, began his personally pivotal 1957 season by winning five games while losing only one during April and May.

On Saturday, June 1, in Philadelphia, Sanford shut out the perennial National League champion Brooklyn Dodgers on two singles, striking out 11 while walking only one. Jack, who faced just 30 batters—three over the minimum—and didn't allow a Dodger to reach second base, called the 3–0 victory "the best game of my life." In truth, the best was yet to come. But clearly, Jack Sanford had arrived.

In his next start, Jack shut out the Chicago Cubs, 1–0, on three hits, again all singles, striking out 13. Two games, two wins, no runs, five hits, and 24 strikeouts. Jack Sanford was 7–1 and fans were finally beginning to talk about him.

"I don't know what I'm doing that's different," Jack would say when the sportswriters, who had pretty much ignored him up until this point, started coming around his locker in the Phillies clubhouse in search of a quote. "But I hope I can keep up whatever I've been doing."

Much of the credit, Jack believed, belonged to Whit Wyatt, who had taught him how to control his curveball. "It took me ten minutes to learn from Wyatt what I hadn't known in seven seasons in the minors," Jack admitted.

Two of Jack's next three starts turned out to be complete game victories over the St. Louis Cardinals and the Milwaukee Braves.

Jack's popularity was growing. And he had no bigger fan in 1957 than his then 13-year-old nephew Jim. "Uncle John and Aunt Patsy called our house and said to my grandmother, 'Can Jim come down to Philadelphia and spend part of the summer with us?'" Jim Sanford recalled. "I took the train by myself from Boston down to Philadelphia. He and my Aunt Patsy picked me up at Penn Station.

Jack, Laura, and Pat

At the time, the Sanford family lived in Prospectville, Pennsylvania, north of Philadelphia. "My mother loved antiques and antique houses and we lived in this really interesting old house that had once been the servants' quarters for a main house that George Washington slept in," recalled daughter Laura. "It was in an old apple orchard so there were apple trees all around. We had a garden. It was real farm country. My grandmother, my father's mother, lived with us some of the time. And John and Nancy were born there."

"Whenever the Phillies were in town, I went to the games with my Uncle John," Jim continued. "I had the run of the locker room and I sat right there in the dugout with the rest of the players. I got a picture of myself and my uncle on the front page of the sports section. Looking back on it now, if I had known where I was and what I was doing, it was any kid's dream world. But you don't realize it at that age.

"He was so nice to our family," Jim said. "He sent us all kinds of stuff. I got my first transistor radio, a nice Motorola, from Uncle John. When he was in Florida for spring training, my family would suddenly get a huge case of oranges. And we'd have no idea where it came from. But it was Uncle John who sent them up. Or we'd get a huge case of bubble gum with baseball cards in it. We wouldn't know where it came from. But he was the one who sent them.

"He gave me my first good baseball glove. It was a MacGregor. It was absolutely beautiful. But it was so friggin heavy, until I got big enough I almost had to tie it onto my hand so it wouldn't fall off. He gave me my first good bat. He was always sending us baseballs and caps.

"I don't know if my Uncle John felt sorry for me or took a liking to me. I was sick when I was four or five. I was in the Children's Hospital for a while. And John was the one who kind of picked me up and got me going. I never was able to play ball like my brothers did but John made sure I was always taken care of, just like I was his son. He made sure I got good grades in school. He made sure I went to college. And when my wife and I got married, he made sure we had a good honeymoon."

~

By the time the 1957 All-Star Game arrived, Sanford was 10–2. And, thanks in no small part to Jack, the Phillies, who had finished 22 games off the pace the year before, were seven games over .500, in fourth place, just four games behind St. Louis. In Sanford's first 15 starts, the Phillies were 13–2.

Of course, Jack was named to the National League All-Star team—the only rookie on a squad that included Hall of Fame greats Hank Aaron, Willie Mays, Stan Musial, Ernie Banks, and Frank Robinson. Sanford was the first Phillies rookie pitcher ever to be named an All-Star.

The 1957 All-Star Game, baseball's Midsummer Classic as it was known in those days, was played on July 9 at Busch Stadium in St. Louis. An effort by Cincinnati fans to stuff the ballot box and stack the NL starting lineup with Redlegs was thwarted by commissioner Ford Frick, who replaced Reds outfielders Gus Bell and Wally Post with Mays and Aaron.

In the sixth inning, with the American League leading 2–0, NL manager Walter Alston sent Sanford to the mound to replace Milwaukee's Lew Burdette. Jack promptly sent his first warm-up pitch sailing all the way to the backstop. But he settled down enough to get the first hitter he faced, Red Sox legend Ted Williams, to fly out to left. The Yankees' Bill Skowron then lined a double to right and, after Sanford advanced Skowron to third on a wild pitch, New York's Yogi Berra singled him home. Sanford then got Boston's Frank Malzone and rival pitcher Billy Loes to ground out, ending the only All-Star appearance of Jack's career. Wally Moon pinch-hit for Sanford in the bottom of the sixth, Larry Jackson replaced Jack on the mound in the seventh, and the AL eventually won the game, 6–5.

When the regular season resumed, the victories continued to pile up as Sanford posted four more complete-game wins by the end of July. On July 15, Jack defeated the St. Louis Cardinals, 6–2, to put the Phillies into a tie for first place—the first time they had sat atop the National League standings that late in a season since 1950, when the Whiz Kids won the pennant.

Everyone was stunned—no one more so than Jack himself. "I can't believe this has happened to me," he declared. "I was nervous in my first start last fall, and I'm still nervous."

At 14–3, with two months left to play, Sanford looked like a cinch to win 20 games—in his first season in the big leagues. Twenty wins is the standard by which all starting pitchers in the major leagues are measured. It is an exclusive club that every starter aspires to join. On August 30, Jack pitched another complete game, raising his record to 17–5 with a full month to play. Jack's mother, Margaret, kidded him, warning him, "Don't do like you did with that violin and stop at nineteen."

But he did. After losing three games in a row in September—Jack blamed his slump on the late summer heat—Sanford closed out the season with a couple of victories over the Dodgers, boosting his season record against Brooklyn to 4–0 and leaving him with a 19–8 record and a 3.08 ERA over 236.2 workhorse innings for the year. Not bad for a rookie who had never won more than 16 games in any one season during his prolonged stint in the minor leagues.

Most surprising of all, perhaps, was Jack's two-to-one strikeouts-to-walks ratio. In his first year in the big leagues, against the best hitters the National League had to offer, Sanford, who had been haunted and held back by wildness wherever he pitched, struck out 188 while walking only 94, leading all major league pitchers in strikeouts. All in all, it was quite an achievement—but a disappointment nonetheless, because Jack had failed to reach 20 wins.

In 1957, future Hall of Famer Warren Spahn of the Milwaukee Braves won 21 games to lead the National League. In the American League, Jim Bunning (Detroit Tigers), who was also headed for Cooperstown, and veteran Billy Pierce (Chicago White Sox) won 20 apiece.

Sanford defeated every team in the National League except the Cincinnati Redlegs at least twice in 1957. Jack, who also topped the NL with a dozen wild pitches, lost all three of his starts against the Reds, twice due to his own wildness and ineffectiveness. Nevertheless, Redlegs manager Birdie Tebbetts came away impressed. "Sanford reminds me of some of the old-time pitchers with that straight overhand stuff of his," said Tebbetts, a savvy former catcher. "He's solid."

Venerable Jimmy Dykes, who had been in the big leagues since 1918, as a player and later as a manager, proclaimed that no pitcher in the league had a faster "hummer" than Jack. St. Louis Cardinals superstar Stan Musial declared, "He can ride a fastball in on a hitter better than anyone since Whitlow Wyatt."

"The Irish are often late in getting their full growth,"

Sanford explained after his breakout rookie season. "I think that's one of the things that happened to me. I never used to be able to throw as hard as I do now. You can see from the records. I never led any league in strikeouts until I got up here."

In part because of Jack's performance, the Phillies' attendance in 1957 soared to 1,146,230—then the second highest mark in franchise history.

Jack was one of the Phillies' promising Fabulous Four Freshmen—Sanford, Ed Bouchee, Harry "The Horse" Anderson, and Chico Fernandez—who rekindled memories of Philly's 1950 Whiz Kids. However, of the four, only Jack lived up to the promise of '57.

Should the Phillies have summoned Sanford to the big leagues sooner? We'll never know. However, in those days the Phillies were not always known for their shrewd judgment when it came to evaluating young talent.

In 1953, while Jack was toiling at AAA Baltimore in the International League, the Phillies passed on signing skinny young high school outfielder Al Kaline and instead lavished a $100,000 bonus on an 18-year-old pitcher named Tom Qualters. Because of Qualters's huge signing bonus, the Phillies were forced to keep him on the bench in the major leagues in '53 when he should have been honing his skills in the minor leagues. Qualters made one big league appearance that year. He faced seven batters, six of whom reached base and scored, giving Qualters an earned-run average for the year of 162.00. Qualters never won a game at the major league level in 34 appearances spread out over several years.

Jack Sanford's salary at the start of the 1957 season is believed to have been $6,000. When he was still on the team on May 15, he received an automatic raise to the major league minimum of $7,500.

At the end of Jack Sanford's surprising first season, after appearing in the All-Star Game, he was voted the National League Rookie of the Year—the first Phillies player to receive that award since it had been instituted in 1947. He also finished a highly respectable 10th in balloting for the NL Most Valuable Player Award by the Baseball Writers Association of America. As a reward, the Phillies reportedly gave Jack a $2,500 bonus, bringing his total compensation for the season to $10,000.

But not everyone believed Sanford was the NL's top rookie in 1957. *The Sporting News* named Jack's teammate, Phillies first baseman Ed Bouchee, who had batted .293 and belted 17 home runs, as its Rookie of the Year. On January 17, 1958, Spokane, Washington, police arrested Bouchee, who pled guilty to two counts of indecent exposure involving children and underwent psychiatric treatment.

At 28, Jack was not the oldest player to be named Rookie of the Year by the BBWAA. That distinction went to Boston Braves outfielder Sam Jethroe, a veteran of the Negro Leagues, who was 33 when he won the award in 1950.

Publicly, Sanford was now being hailed, along with Robin Roberts and Curt Simmons, as a member of the Phillies' pitching Big Three. When Jack's contract for the 1958 season arrived in the mail, he saw that he would be receiving a substantial raise, reportedly more than doubling his basic '57 salary to $18,000. That may seem a pitiful amount by today's standards, but Roberts, the highest-paid player on the team, was only making $37,500 and future Hall of Famer Richie Ashburn was making $30,000.

In assessing the Phillies' outlook for 1958, *Sports Illustrated* declared: "Out of the minor leagues last year popped three young men, all right-handers, all impressive. Best of the lot was Jack Sanford, who won 19 games and the Rookie of the Year Award. Sanford, who struck out 188 batters, throws a fastball that looks about half the size of other men's fastballs."

Nevertheless, in spite of the nice raise and all of the words of praise, Jack still harbored doubts. "I don't think I ever really had confidence until last year," Sanford said in the 1958 *Saturday Evening Post* article, which was entitled "Baseball's Oldest Youngster." "And having one good year up here doesn't convince me."

BALL | **STRIKE** | **OUT** |

FAIR-PLAY by TRANSLUX

	1	2	3	4	5	6	7	8	9	TOTAL
VISITOR										
HOME										

HORST TRADE I EVER MADE

The 1958 Philadelphia Phillies plunged to last place in the National League standings. And Jack Sanford sank with them. His earned-run average soared from an impressive 3.08 in 1957 to an unsightly 4.44 in '58. His strikeouts dropped from nearly six per game to fewer than three. In 1958 Jack won just 10 games while losing 13. And he completed just seven games, compared to 15 the season before.

In baseball parlance, that is what is known as a "sophomore slump," and it affects an alarmingly large number of players, especially pitchers—particularly those pitchers who win the Rookie of the Year Award. Historically, the statistics of pitchers who are feted as

ROY have declined an average of 33 percent in their second season.

Apparently, the Phillies didn't take that into account. Manager Mayo Smith, the man who gave Jack his chance to pitch in the big leagues, was fired midway through the 1958 collapse and the Phillies brought back their old "Whiz Kids" skipper, Eddie Sawyer, in a futile effort to reprise the team's 1950 success.

Meanwhile, as Sanford's stock dropped, the Phillies' opinion of their newest rookie surprise, Ray Semproch (13–11), rose. When the time came for the Phillies front office to seek excuses for their tumble into the NL cellar, Jack became a convenient, conspicuous scapegoat.

On December 3, 1958, during baseball's annual winter meetings, the Phillies abruptly wrote Jack off as a one-year wonder, making him the first pitcher from either league to be traded away one year after being hailed as Rookie of the Year. It was typical of the way things had gone for Jack up until that point in his baseball career.

Hoping to get some value for him while he still could, Phillies general manager Roy Hamey shipped Sanford cross-country to the San Francisco Giants in exchange for backup catcher Valmy Thomas and screwball-specialist Ruben Gomez, whose main claim to fame was the fact that he had shut out the Los Angeles Dodgers, 8–0, on April 15, 1958, in the first major league baseball game ever played on the West Coast.

Publicly, the Phillies justified the deal by patting themselves on the back for acquiring an intact major league-caliber battery. However, there may have been more to that trade than first met the eye. Cuban-born shortstop Chico Fernandez, the Phillies' first black player, had been the only minority on the squad during most of the 1958 season. But he had increasingly become a target of the infamous Philadelphia boo-birds and the Phillies front office was under pressure to increase the minority presence on the ballclub. Although Gomez was Puerto Rican and Thomas had been born in St. Thomas in the U.S. Virgin Islands, both players were considered black in the parlance of the day. The trade, at least temporarily, took Hamey and the front office off the hook.

Nevertheless, the swap was a steal for the Giants and a slap in the face to Jack. Giants pitching coach Bill Posedel, who had been a member of the Phillies coaching staff the year before and therefore knew Sanford well, called it "the best deal the Giants could have made.

"I'm surprised Roy Hamey of the Phillies went through with the deal," Posedel added.

A month later, in January 1959, Hamey himself was let go when his contract expired and was replaced as GM by John Quinn, whom the Phillies lured away from Lou Perini's Milwaukee Braves.

After leaving Philadelphia against his will, Sanford

pitched nine more years and won an additional 116 games in the big leagues before retiring following the 1967 season. Meanwhile, over the course of those same nine years, three of which Gomez spent pitching in Mexico, Ruben, who was known in his native Puerto Rico as "El Divino Loco" (The Divine Madman), won just five major league games, lost 17, and worked a total of just over 200 innings. Gomez always claimed the Giants promised to "bring me right back." But they never did. Thomas, the first player from the Virgin Islands to reach the big leagues, lasted just one year in Philadelphia and played only 101 games with three different teams over the next three seasons, collecting a total of 47 hits. "Going to Philly," Thomas later lamented, "was like going to jail."

No wonder Phillies owner Bob Carpenter, scion of the DuPont fortune and the youngest club president in baseball history when he took control of the family baseball team in 1943, would later call the decision to dump Jack Sanford "the worst trade I ever made." As Bill Libby wrote of Sanford in *Sport* magazine, "He worked seven years in the minors, he was 28 years old before he made the majors. Then he won 19 games for a last-place club and was Rookie of the Year. And a year later, he was sent packing, traded to the other end of the country for a couple of nobodies." After discarding Jack, the Phillies would remain buried in the NL basement until 1962.

Jack was as disgusted with the Phillies for giving up on him as he was disappointed by his own performance in 1958. And he was determined to prove the Phillies wrong. Jack tipped the scales at 191 pounds when he reported to the Giants' spring training camp in Phoenix, Arizona—21 pounds less than he weighed at the end of the 1958 season. He credited eight days of mineral baths and massages at nearby Buckhorn Springs for the return to his rookie year fitness.

The sudden swap and the move west was hard on Jack's family, too. "I don't remember the trade," said daughter Laura who was three years old at the time. "But I do remember going to spring training in Arizona when I was in the first grade. I didn't have to go to school. I had a tutor three days a week. It was really fun. We stayed in a place that had a pool. My grandmother [Jack's mother] was with us. After spring training, we went out to California and I went back to school. And I was definitely not in synch with what was going on in that school. That was the last year that we went to spring training as a family. It was just too hard for me, going to different schools."

~

In addition to Jack, the 1959 Giants bolstered their pitching staff by acquiring veteran Sam Jones, who had led the National League in strikeouts three times. Their starting rotation also included longtime ace Johnny

Antonelli and 20-year-old Mike McCormick. As *Sports Illustrated* noted with some skepticism in the magazine's preseason analysis: "Newcomers Sam Jones and Jack Sanford could erase the pitching weak spot but, don't forget, they each lost 13 games last year."

Offensively, the Giants featured the great Willie Mays along with rookie Orlando Cepeda in a lineup that would soon include slugging young first baseman Willie McCovey. All three men would end up in baseball's Hall of Fame.

Facing the St. Louis Cardinals in his second start as a Giant, Sanford walked three batters in the first inning, hit another, unleashed a wild pitch, and gave up a run on a sacrifice fly. Then he held the Cardinals hitless until Stan Musial led off the seventh with a single. It was the only hit Jack allowed all day in winning, 8–1.

Jack proceeded to win four in a row and the Giants moved into first place on July 4. They led the National League by three games on September 9, when Sanford beat the Pittsburgh Pirates, 7–2, for his 13th win of the season. The Giants continued to hang on to first place and led by two games on September 17 after Jack bested future Hall of Famer Warren Spahn and the reigning National League champion Milwaukee Braves, 13–6. Sanford and the Giants appeared headed for the World Series.

But Giants manager Bill Rigney panicked down the

stretch and leaned almost exclusively on his top four starters during the final two weeks of the season as the team lost seven of eight to blow the pennant to the archrival Los Angeles Dodgers by three games. At one point, Jack was called upon to pitch three times in six days. "When [Rigney] smelled that pennant, he just worked Sam [Jones] to death," recalled Giants relief ace Stu Miller.

Nevertheless, Sanford regained his rookie-year form in 1959, winning 15 while losing 12 and lowering his ERA to 3.16.

In 1960, Jack led the league in shutouts with six and completed 11 games, but his record dipped to 12–14 and his ERA rose to 3.82. He also led the league in wild pitches with 15.

And Jack's temper again reared its ugly head. When 66-year-old manager Tom Clancy Sheehan, who had replaced Bill Rigney midway through the 1960 season, marched out to the mound to take Sanford out of a game in the middle of the fourth inning on September 7 in Milwaukee, Jack didn't bother waiting for his manager to arrive, as pitchers are traditionally supposed to do. Instead, Jack stalked off the hill, passing his burly manager halfway between the mound and the Giants dugout.

"[Sheehan] chugs along with his head down and Sanford knows he's going out of the game," relief pitcher

Stu Miller recalled. "As soon as Santa [Sheehan] takes that first step, [Jack] just shoots by him to the dugout." Observers insisted Sanford was going faster than the rather rotund Sheehan was coming. "By the time Santa gets out to the mound, he looks around and says, 'Where the hell is my pitcher?' " Miller continued. "Sanford was already in the dugout. [Sheehan] never saw him go by."

"[Jack] is such an intense competitor, sometimes he flips his trolley," explained Sheehan, who immediately fined Jack $200.

The Giants were in second place, eight games over .500 when Rigney was fired—reportedly because he insisted on playing Eddie Bressoud at shortstop rather than owner Horace Stoneham's personal favorite, Andre Rodgers. Under Sheehan, a career minor league manager, coach, and scout—and, reportedly, Stoneham's drinking buddy—they finished fifth.

"We laughed all the way down to the lowest point in the standings we could find," Stu Miller recalled. "We just laughed at that man. [Sheehan] didn't even have a uniform for four days. I think Omar the Tentmaker had to make it." At the end of the season, Sheehan quietly went back to scouting.

Jack, always money conscious, perhaps because he had had so little in his life, expected a raise after the 1960 season. He also wanted that $200 fine that Sheehan had imposed rescinded. Instead, the first contract that the

Giants sent him that winter called for a cut in pay. Jack claimed it was the first time he had been asked to take a pay cut in his 13 years as a professional ballplayer. "I'll wrap that contract around my fastball and throw it right back at them," he bristled. Eventually, Jack relented and signed. He had no other choice. There was no free agency in those days. Reportedly, the Giants also tried to trade Sanford during that offseason but found no serious takers.

In 1961, Jack won 13 games, losing nine. But his ERA jumped to 4.22 and he struck out just 112 batters in 217 innings. That winter, the Giants front office, believing Jack's career was in decline, decided to jettison him by placing him in the expansion draft, the grab bag of discards and has-beens who would be available for $75,000 per player to fill the rosters of the newly created New York Mets and Houston Colt .45s.

To Jack, that would have been the ultimate insult, yet another slap in the face. However, Alvin Dark, the Giants' captain and shortstop in the 1950s who had taken over as their manager in 1961, talked the brass into hanging onto Jack. Both Dark and San Francisco would soon be glad that he did.

```
┌─────────────────────────────────────────────────────────┐
│  BALL □   STRIKE 2   OUT □                               │
├─────────────────────────────────────────────────────────┤
│ FAIR-PLAY   1  2  3  4  5  6  7  8  9   TOTAL            │
│ by TRANSLUX                                              │
│ VISITOR  □ □ □ □ │ □ □    □ │                            │
│ HOME     □ □ □ □ □ □ □     □                             │
├─────────────────────────────────────────────────────────┤
│              I'VE WON TWENTY!                            │
└─────────────────────────────────────────────────────────┘
```

By 1962 the San Francisco Giants had rebuilt their pitching staff, acquiring left-handed starters Billy Pierce and Billy O'Dell to go along with Jack Sanford, future Hall of Famer Juan Marichal, and Mike McCormick. But the '62 season didn't begin particularly well for Jack and there were times when Dark regretted going to bat for Sanford the previous fall when the Giants brass had wanted to discard Jack in the expansion draft.

During spring training, Jack, now 32, struggled and complained that the ball seemed to grow "bigger and heavier with each pitch." In the first two and a half months of the season, during which Jack won six and lost six, it sometimes looked like he was throwing balloons toward the plate.

FRISCO FIRST LINERS
Mike McCormick • Jack Sanford • Billy O'Dell

On May 28, in a "Flash Crash," the stock market lost $19 billion—the biggest plunge since 1929, the year Jack was born.

And on June 8, after leading the league for all but nine days since the beginning of the season, the Giants dropped into second place. The Giants were notorious for slumping in June, leading to the phrase "June Swoon," and inspiring famed sports columnist Jim Murray of the *Los Angeles Times* to write: "A business executive is standing in his office and chatting to his secretary. Suddenly, a falling figure shoots past the window. 'Oh, oh,' says the man, glancing at his chronometer. 'It must be June. There go the Giants.'" If Jack read that column, he undoubtedly didn't think it was very funny.

On June 13, Sanford lost, 5–0, to the Cincinnati Reds, in a game in which he lasted just five innings. It was Jack's second five-inning start and second loss in a row. "I guess I got mad after that," he recalled. It would be September 15 before Jack would lose again, as he reeled off a near-record 16 victories in a row.

Major League Baseball held two All-Star Games in 1962. By the time the second exhibition rolled around, on July 30, Jack had won seven straight, raising his record to 13–6. Why National League manager Fred Hutchinson left Jack off his pitching staffs for both games, although a total of 10 hurlers were picked for the two games, remains a mystery. Obviously, Hutchinson didn't believe in Jack Sanford, selecting Turk Farrell, with his 7–13 record, Johnny Podres (7–7), and Bob Purkey (8–6) instead.

On September 11, Jack defeated the Pittsburgh Pirates, 2–0, for his 22nd win of the season and his 16th consecutive victory. "This is ridiculous," Jack declared. "No one wins sixteen in a row. Sure, a good pitcher might expect to win five or six in a row. But then bad luck catches up to him. Sixteen? That's ridiculous. I don't care who you are or how lucky you are, you don't do it. Ah, well," he added, "I'll take 'em as they come."

Sanford's 16 consecutive wins left him just three short of the modern-day major league record of 19, set by Hall of Famer and vaudeville performer Rube Marquard of the New York Giants in 1912. Only

Marquard and Roy Face of the Pittsburgh Pirates, with 17 straight in 1959, have won more consecutive games in the modern era than Sanford.

Nevertheless, Jack insisted he was not impressed. "I have no idea who won nineteen in a row and I don't care," he grumbled, after his streak came to an end with a 5–1 loss to the Pirates on September 15. "A record doesn't mean anything to me."

In 1957, Jack's rookie season with the Phillies, he had just missed winning 20 games, finishing with 19. In 1962, with the Giants, he reached the 20-win mark on September 3 with a 7–3 victory over the Los Angeles Dodgers. As former pitcher Jim Bouton wrote in *Ball Four*, his controversial kiss-and-tell exposé: "If you had a pill that would guarantee a pitcher twenty wins, but might take five years off his life, he'd take it."

To Jack, winning 20 definitely was a big deal. "In the fifth inning we had a lead and I started to think, 'I've won twenty!'" Sanford declared. "I wish I could stuff and mount this game for my trophy case. It's one I'd like to look at over and over again."

Laura Sanford recalled listening to the game on the radio with her mother. "It was so exciting," she said.

"I'm glad it was against the Dodgers," Jack continued. "One like this is worth two against anyone else. You know what I'm thinking? I'm thinking, 'God, I'm using up all my luck.'"

During the 1962 season, Giants manager Al Dark seemed to know exactly when to take Jack out of a game and bring in junk ball reliever Stu Miller, who had been blown off the mound at Candlestick Park during the 1961 All-Star Game, to save the win. One San Francisco sportswriter tabbed Sanford "the composer of the Unfinished Symphony."

"What a pitcher needs is good luck and a strong bullpen," admitted Jack, who could no longer blow enemy hitters away with his fastball the way he did earlier in his career, but who had added a slider to his arsenal. That gave batters, who might have been tempted to sit on Sanford's fastball, another pitch to worry about.

"I've been lucky," Jack admitted. "I was lucky in 1957 when I won those nineteen for the Phils. Thirteen of them were by one run. Is that lucky?" Actually, only seven of Sanford's 19 wins in '57 came by one run, but his point was well taken.

Sanford also gave much of the credit for his 1962 success to his favorite catcher, Tom Haller. "You don't suppose I could have done all this by myself, do you?" Jack said.

Because Sanford put so much effort into every pitch, especially his fastballs, he frequently tired in the later innings, especially as he got older. He was no longer the same pitcher he had been in 1957 when, as a rookie, he completed 15 of his 33 starts with the Phillies. Adhering to Dark's admonition to throw as hard as he could for as long as he could, Jack completed just six of his 20 starts during his 16-game winning streak. Jack won his final two starts in 1962, including an 11–5 victory over the Houston Astros that helped the Giants catch the first-place Los Angeles Dodgers, to finish the season with a career-best record of 24–7. In addition, he struck out 147 batters, the most since his sensational rookie season with the Phillies in 1957, and posted a 3.43 ERA.

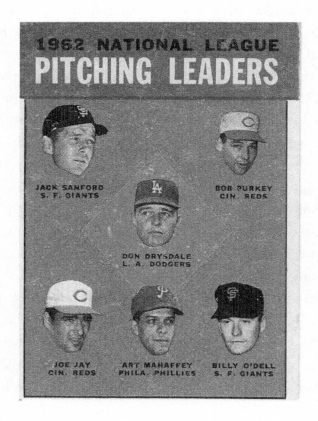

"Jack was almost unhittable that year," teammate Don Larsen said.

He also completed 13 games—again his best effort since '57.

In the words of Giants pitching coach Larry Jansen, Jack had become "a pitcher" rather than "a thrower."

"Jack Sanford was a great pitcher at his best," Juan Marichal, a Hall of Famer, wrote in his autobiography,

Juan Marichal: My Journey from the Dominican Republic to Cooperstown. "He had good control and a good slider, and he knew how to pitch. He was somebody you wanted to watch and learn from. He was that kind of pitcher."

"He realizes his temper has hurt him a lot and he's maybe controlled it a little better," offered teammate Harvey Kuenn, who was himself named Rookie of Year with the Detroit Tigers in 1953 when he led the American League in hits with 209. "He's concentrating more and he's smarter because he's been around longer. But the big things are the control, the new pitch [the slider], and the things he's always had: a lot of fight and willingness to work hard. He's a brooder, sure, but it's his mistakes he's brooding about so he won't make them again."

As usual, Jack was honest about his shortcomings. "I used to go out there and just throw it," he said. "Now I have an idea what I want to do with it and I'm getting so I can do it. And I've got better control. I throw some curveballs and a few changeups. But mostly I just fire the fast one. I'm a dart thrower. I'm still a fastball pitcher. That's my big pitch. I throw as hard as I can for as long as I can."

In spite of all Jack's success and accomplishments in 1962, according to sportswriter Bill Libby, he "as usual brooded through the season, seeing things only as they hurt him, turning that ice-blue look on an unfriendly world. It was a magnificent season but only occasionally would you know it to look at him."

Walter Bingham, writing in *Sports Illustrated*, echoed those sentiments. "The angry man of the Giants staff is Jack Sanford, one of the Bay Area's favorite television characters," wrote Bingham. "Standing on the mound, getting the sign from the catcher, Sanford scowls and grimaces, and the camera picks it all up."

"He's better than Matt Dillon," said one TV viewer, obviously a fan of the popular show *Gunsmoke*.

"No one loses himself more in a game than Sanford does," said Alvin Dark. "After a game, win or lose, Dark gave Jack permission to go unwind. He did not have to have a curfew. And I had permission to go with him. And he'd unwind all right. He'd unwind a few," said Jack's road roommate Stu Miller.

After one night game in which Sanford was the losing pitcher, Dark told the Giants to skip batting practice the next day, relax and report to the ballpark at noon, an hour before game time. Nevertheless, Sanford arrived at nine in the morning and sat on his stool, alone in the locker room, scowling for three hours. When Dark eventually wandered by to offer his sympathy on the loss, Sanford merely stared at the floor.

"Jack wasn't the easiest guy to know," admitted Tom Haller, Sanford's catcher of choice. Haller added that Jack was from "the wrong side of the tracks," and, like many

Boston Irishmen, had to "battle for everything in his life."

Grumpy or not, however, Jack was a steady winner. The Giants, in second place since July 8, won six of their final nine games to finish the regular season tied for first with the Los Angeles Dodgers, who lost 10 of their last 13, including four on the final weekend, to force a best-two-out-of-three playoff.

Both teams, bitter West Coast rivals, had won 101 games while losing 61, as the Giants' starting rotation of Sanford, Juan Marichal, Billy O'Dell, and Billy Pierce accounted for 77 wins compared to 68 for the Dodgers' quartet of Don Drysdale, Sandy Koufax, Johnny Podres, and Stan Williams.

San Francisco, behind veteran lefty Billy Pierce, won the Monday opener of the three-game showdown against the Dodgers, 8–0, over Sandy Koufax as Pierce tossed a three-hitter and Willie Mays homered twice. After the game, Koufax, who had been called upon to pitch because Drysdale and Podres had both pitched on the weekend, trying to stop the Dodgers' nosedive and clinch the pennant, admitted, "I had nothing at all."

In those days, the groundskeepers at San Francisco's Candlestick Park were often accused of watering the base paths to slow down Dodgers speedster Maury Wills. The 1962 playoffs were no exception. "One more squirt and the Red Cross would have declared a disaster area and begun to evacuate the Dodgers by rowboat," wrote Jim Murray in the *LA Times*.

The next afternoon in Los Angeles, Sanford, fighting a head cold, matched pitches with the Dodgers' 25-game winner and future Hall of Famer Don Drysdale. Drysdale had pitched three times in the previous eight days, but, with the Dodgers' backs to the wall, the big right-hander convinced manager Walter Alston that he was ready to go.

The matchup had been billed as a pitchers' duel but it turned out to be just the opposite. In the top half of the sixth inning, with the game still scoreless, it was obvious Drysdale was pitching on fumes. Giants catcher Tom Haller walked and Jose Pagan doubled him to third. With one away, and Sanford at the plate, Giants manager Al Dark signaled for a suicide squeeze bunt. With Haller heading full-speed toward home plate, Jack squared at the last second and dropped a bunt down directly in front of Drysdale. The Dodgers' pitcher fielded the ball, then slipped and fell to the ground. Haller scored the game's first run, Pagan advanced to third, and Sanford was safe at first.

By the time Sanford strolled back to the mound to begin the bottom of the sixth with a two-hitter working, having allowed just four base runners up to that point, he had a comfortable 5–0 lead. But when Jack walked the Dodgers' leadoff hitter, Jim Gilliam, Dark immediately bolted out of the Giants dugout. Apparently believing Sanford was also out of gas, Dark replaced him with the usually reliable changeup artist Stu Miller, who was affectionately known in the Giants clubhouse as "The Killer Moth." "Sanford was suffering from a cold and he was pooped," Dark explained after the game.

With Jack now out of the game, all he could do was watch helplessly from the dugout, while the San Francisco bullpen that had been so effective so many times during the regular season served up seven runs on four hits, two walks, and a hit batsman that half inning as the Dodgers sent 10 men to the plate. The Giants eventually blew the ballgame, 8–7.

"That second playoff game in Los Angeles in October had a lot to do with me getting traded," recalled Miller, who was dealt to the Baltimore Orioles in a multiplayer swap that offseason.

What's more, Miller had quite a different explanation for Sanford's unexpected early exit. "We're ahead 5–0 in the sixth inning when Sanford decides he's had enough, which Dark gave him as a prerogative, that he could take himself out," Miller recalled. "So he's had enough. So who does Dark bring in but his ace reliever, naturally, to sew up the pennant. Well, by the time that inning is over, they're ahead, 7–5. I had goat horns sprouting out all over me.

"Oh, man, I had no idea why I didn't do that job. I

felt good. I don't know. I think it's a sure thing I finished my career as a Giant that day.

"I never asked Jack Sanford why he took himself out," Miller continued. "I'd like to ask him why. He was my roommate and I still didn't ask him why. Jack was a very high-strung guy. He kept everything to himself. But he was wound tighter than a string. Jack won twenty-four games that year. And I probably saved sixteen of them.

"I never saw him go out of a game like that, except in '62. He was a great competitor. But Dark made a mistake and said, 'All I need is five or six good ones from you,' " Miller recalled. "And Jack said, 'Well, that's all I'm going to give him.' I don't think Dark wanted it that way."

Game two of the 1962 playoffs, which saw the two teams employ 42 players, including 13 pitchers, lasted four hours and 18 minutes, the longest nine-inning contest in major league history until April 30, 1996, when it took the Yankees and Orioles four hours and 21 minutes to play a game.

Don Larsen, best remembered for pitching a perfect game on behalf of the Yankees against the Dodgers in the 1956 World Series, beat the Dodgers again, 6–4, pitching in relief of Juan Marichal in the deciding third game of the playoff. The Giants rallied for four runs in the ninth inning to advance to the World Series.

At long last, after languishing in the minors for seven years, and spending six seasons struggling for recognition in the majors, Jack was finally headed for baseball's ultimate destination, the World Series.

"You never forget a year like '62," Al Dark declared. Jack Sanford certainly wouldn't.

```
BALL 2    STRIKE 0    OUT 0
```

FAIR-PLAY by TRANSLUX	1	2	3	4	5	6	7	8	9	TOTAL	
VISITOR	☐	☐	☐	☐	☐	☐	☐	☐		☐	
HOME	☐	☐	☐	☐	☐	☐	☐	☐		☐	☐

I LOST. THAT'S ALL. I JUST LOST.

Even upon baseball's biggest stage, with a 24-win season that included a near-record 16 consecutive victories under his belt, Jack Sanford was still haunted by his history and his lack of confidence.

On the eve of the 1962 World Series, a reporter asked Sanford if he was nervous.

"(Bleeping), yes," Jack replied with a characteristic blend of candor and profanity. "Oh, (bleep), (bleeping), yes.

"But one thing, one (bleeping) thing for sure, they're not going to send me down again, no matter how (bleeping) bad I do."

The Giants, with five future Hall of Famers—Willie Mays, Orlando Cepeda, Juan Marichal, Willie McCovey, and Gaylord Perry—on their roster, boasted a higher team batting average and had hit more home runs and triples during the regular season than the vaunted Yankees.

Nevertheless, Jack's exhausted Giants entered the 1962 Series at a distinct disadvantage, having had to battle down the stretch to catch Los Angeles, then dispose of the Dodgers in a hard-fought three-game playoff, before they could advance to face the rested and powerful Yanks.

The Yankees, who had won the American League pennant by five games over the Minnesota Twins, had flown to San Francisco after their regular season ended and held a leisurely workout at Candlestick Park while the Giants were dealing with the Dodgers.

With the World Series scheduled to begin in less than 15 hours, Sanford and the victorious Giants landed back in San Francisco on the evening of Wednesday, October 2, in the midst of a raucous victory celebration. Seventy-five thousand joyous Giants fans waited at the airport for the team's arrival, clogging terminals, runways, and area highways, hugging, and dancing, and honking car horns. In San Francisco's financial district, ticker tape and torn telephone books were tossed out of office windows. As the Giants team bus tried to get out of the airport, jubilant fans rocked the bus and tried to break the windows to touch the players. "That was as scared as I've ever been," admitted catcher Ed Bailey.

The party continued until well past midnight. As

author Roger Angell, who had flown from Los Angeles to San Francisco on the airplane chartered to transport the baseball writers covering the postseason, wrote, the fans "all had the shiny-eyed, stunned, exhausted expression of a bride at her wedding reception."

For the Giants, after their regular season comeback and their triumph in the playoff, the World Series seemed almost anticlimactic. Two hours before the start of the first Series game, a drained Willie Mays, who would be playing in his third World Series, was sitting in silence in front of his locker when a reporter asked, "Are you as tense before this game as you were in 1951 and 1954?"

"Man," Mays replied, "after that playoff in Los Angeles, I'm all out of tense." Throughout the Series, Mays, who in September had collapsed on the bench from exhaustion and had to be transported to the hospital, kept moaning, "I'm so tired, I can't wait for this thing to end."

The Giants' fatigue showed in the Series opener as Whitey Ford, the 1961 American League Cy Young Award winner making his customary Game One start for the Yankees, whipped them, 6–2, at San Francisco's Candlestick Park.

From the Giants dugout, Jack watched the Bronx Bombers at bat. "I remember watching [Mickey] Mantle swing the bat," Sanford recalled years later in an interview with the *Palm Beach Post*. "Billy O'Dell was pitching that one for us and you could actually hear [Mantle's] bat, like when you swing a driver. And I knew I had to face him the next day.

"A lot of guys say, once they throw the first pitch they're able to relax. It was never that way for me. I always had to work for nine innings."

Before his first start, in Game Two of the World Series, Sanford, whose uniform number 33 matched his age, decided to call former Phillies teammate Robin Roberts to get a scouting report on the Yankees. Roberts, who was headed for the Hall of Fame, had pitched in the American League for the Baltimore Orioles during the 1962 season and Jack hoped to get some valuable inside information. But Roberts's telephone was unlisted and Sanford had difficulty tracking down his old teammate. "Rather than go to a lot of trouble to get it, I said the hell with it," Jack said later.

1962 World Series, Game 2, First Pitch

Sanford, still suffering from a bad cold and making his third start in seven days of both regular season and playoff, shut out the mighty Yankees, including Mickey Mantle, the American League's Most Valuable Player, and Roger Maris, who had broken Babe Ruth's home run record the year before. Sanford allowed just three hits for a clutch 2–0 complete game victory over New York's Ralph Terry, squaring the Series at one win apiece, and making Sanford the first pitcher to shut the mighty Yankees out in a World Series game in four years.

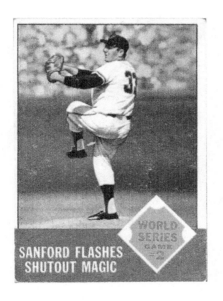

SANFORD FLASHES
SHUTOUT MAGIC

WORLD SERIES GAME #2

Mantle, Tom Tresh, and Clete Boyer collected the Yanks' three hits and Sanford also walked three while striking out six. Mantle, who went one-for-four when he doubled after two men were out in the ninth inning, was the only Yankee runner to reach second base as New York hit just six pitches from Sanford out of the infield.

"I struck [Mantle] out twice and had two strikes on him in the ninth," Jack bragged to the *Palm Beach Post* nearly three decades later. In fact, Mantle had popped out to short and third and grounded out in his first three at-bats against Sanford in Game Two. But 26 years tend to play tricks on a man's memory.

Yogi Berra, the Yankees' free-swinging Hall of Fame slugger, complained that Sanford hadn't given the Yanks anything to hit.

"No one ever pitched a better game," praised Giants manager Alvin Dark.

Jack and Alvin Dark

Sanford agreed, calling it the best game of his life. "I can remember almost every pitch," Jack declared three decades later. "I tried to pitch inside on [Mickey] Mantle and low and away on [Roger] Maris." Jack also went out of his way to praise his catcher in that game, Tom Haller. "There's the guy who will be the take-charge guy of this club within the next couple of years," Jack predicted.

"We didn't know Jack Sanford very well," Yankees manager Ralph Houk said at the time. "But we figured he had to be good with his record. You've got to give him a lot of credit. I thought he moved the ball around good."

As Roy Terrell, writing in *Sports Illustrated*, put it: "[Whitey] Ford pitched well [in Game One on Thursday] but no better than Ralph Terry [in Game Two] on Friday. The only trouble was that Terry ran into Jack Sanford on what Sanford later evaluated as his greatest day. The Boston Irishman, who once worked as a chauffeur for Lou Perini of the Braves and spent seven years rattling around the minor leagues, went into the game with 24 National League victories, a bad cold and only two days' rest. He came out of the game with a cold and a magnificent three-hitter for his first World Series win."

Jack admitted he was so nervous that his hand shook throughout the game. "I was shaking all over," he confessed after the game. "I was nervous at the start and nervous at the finish. About like I felt in my first game as a rookie."

"The [head] cold didn't bother me," Jack later said, between sniffles. "What did I do for it? I blew my nose."

An out-of-town reporter, unfamiliar with Jack and searching for a unique angle, asked, "How many times did you blow your nose during the game?"

Sanford stared in silence at the reporter until another writer defused the impending explosion with a more conventional question.

The two teams split Games Three and Four at Yankee Stadium in New York, leaving baseball's first coast-to-coast Series tied at 2–2.

Jack was scheduled to start Game Five of the Series, also in New York, but it was delayed a day by rain. The wet weather didn't do anything for Jack's lingering head cold, or for his frame of mind. "I don't like it; it was a big letdown," he admitted when asked about the rainout. "With my kind of temperament, I have to crank myself up for a game like this. Now I've got to do it all over again."

To compound the disappointment, Jack's wife and several members of his family were in New York for the game. Jack's nephew Jim was at all three of the games in New York. "Uncle John introduced me to a lot of people," Jim recalled. "I met Willie Mays, Willie McCovey, all of the Alous, Juan Marichal. I met Whitey Ford, Yogi Berra, Casey Stengel, and I met Mickey Mantle."

When the fifth game finally arrived, Jack lost, 5–3, despite allowing just six hits—one a bunt and another a bloop single off the glove of shortstop Jose Pagan—and striking out 10. With the score tied at 2–2, Sanford fanned Yankees pitcher Ralph Terry to begin the eighth inning, but served up singles to Tony Kubek and Bobby Richardson. Al Dark marched to the mound but allowed Jack to remain in the game. Next up for the Yankees was rookie Tom Tresh. "I tried for a strike on the outside corner, but it was a fastball right in the middle and that was it," Jack explained. Tresh blasted a three-run homer into the right-field seats. The Yankees' other two runs had come on a wild pitch by Sanford and catcher Tom Haller's passed ball.

The World Series returned to San Francisco but three days of rain, the remnants of Typhoon Freda which had struck the West Coast, washed out the Series until Monday, October 15. Although damage was heaviest in the Pacific Northwest, the record rainfall caused major flooding and mudslides in the Bay Area, where five people died due to the storms. It was the longest World Series delay since 1911, when the showdown between the Philadelphia Athletics and New York Giants was interrupted for six days by rain.

"Stretched out over seven games and 13 days," wrote the great wordsmith Red Smith in analyzing the '62 Series, "it had everything but continuity."

The torrential downpours forced the two teams to travel to Modesto, California, to work out and put the Giants, who were on the brink of elimination, even further on edge. And, although no one could have realized it at the time, the delay, and the change it would allow Giants manager Alvin Dark to make, would impact Jack Sanford for the rest of his life.

"We should have won the World Series," Willie Mays later told author Glenn Dickey. "We had just as good a team as the Yankees. We had the pitching and we felt we had the better team, but when we had to go to Modesto to work out, it was kind of a letdown."

In addition to its infamous wind, Candlestick Park was notorious for its poor drainage. In an effort to dry the field, Giants owner Horace Stoneham rented three helicopters to hover overhead.

In Game Six, Orlando Cepeda went three-for-four, knocking in two runs, and vintage lefty Billy Pierce held the Yankees to three hits to even the Series once again, 5–2, and set up a winner-take-all Game Seven.

The World Series in the early 1960s, before the advent of interleague play, back when all the games were played during the daytime, was an even bigger deal than it is today. When a Series reached a Game Seven, the whole country stopped whatever it was doing, whether that was work or school or play, to watch.

In '62, that Game Seven showdown again featured

Jack Sanford against Ralph Terry, a rematch made possible by the three days of rain which allowed both managers to reshuffle their pitching rotations.

En route to the ballpark aboard the Yankees team bus, Terry heard radio broadcaster Joe Garagiola predict the Giants would win the World Series because Terry would choke. On the field before the game, Terry, the goat of the 1960 World Series when he served up a historic walk-off home run to the Pittsburgh Pirates' Bill Mazeroski, confronted Garagiola about his comments.

Terry, who had won 23 games for the Yankees during the '62 season, was eager to atone for his Series implosion two years earlier, and he took a perfect game into the sixth inning against the Giants and a two-hit shutout into the ninth.

It was Sanford who broke up Terry's no-hitter with a sixth-inning single to right-center after the Yankees' right-hander had retired 17 Giants in a row.

With the wicked Candlestick Park winds off San Francisco Bay gusting up to 40 miles per hour, Sanford was nearly as sharp as Terry on the mound, holding the Yankees to seven hits over the first seven innings.

As renowned sports columnist Jim Murray of the *Los Angeles Times* wrote: "The game had all the offensive fury of a pillow fight. When the wind blows in, as it did Tuesday, Candlestick Park is a maximum-security stockade for pitchers. A prisoner could get out of

Alcatraz easier than a ball could get over that wall of wind."

New York's only run came on a bases-loaded double play in the fifth inning. Bill Skowron and Clete Boyer singled and Sanford walked Terry to load the bases. The Giants, convinced one run wouldn't be enough to win the game, conceded the run by playing their infield back and Skowron crossed the plate as Tony Kubek grounded into double play.

"I had probably the best control of my life," Jack recalled years later. "But I walked Terry for some reason. Then Kubek hit into a double play and Skowron scored."

Meanwhile, the wind was a challenge for both pitchers. "You'd throw one curveball and it might break six inches," said Terry, who was signed by the Yankees when he was 18 by Tom Greenwade, the same scout who discovered Mickey Mantle. "Another one might break two feet."

Jack was replaced by Billy O'Dell in the eighth inning when the Yankees again loaded the bases with nobody out on a throwing error by Pagan and singles by Tresh and Mantle. O'Dell needed only five pitches to get Roger Maris to ground out and Elston Howard to bounce into a double play, leaving the Yankees still with a precarious one-run lead.

The Giants' biggest threat of the game came in the bottom of the ninth when pinch hitter Matty Alou dragged a bunt single past the mound. Terry struck out both Matty's brother, Felipe Alou, and Chuck Hiller. But Willie Mays, with a chance to replicate Bill Mazeroski's 1960 homer, sliced a double down the right-field line. "I was going for the bomb, trying to hit it out of the park," Mays later admitted.

Alou, representing the tying run, stopped at third as Maris and cutoff man Bobby Richardson relayed the ball home. Given the soggy condition of the field after all of the rain, most observers agreed Alou would have been out if Giants third base coach Whitey Lockman had not thrown up the stop sign.

Had Mays been the runner trying to score, Lockman's decision, the result of the play, and the outcome of the game and the World Series, might have been far different. "If it had been Willie Mays running, he'd have run over the catcher if he had to in order to score," declared Giants manager Al Dark. "There would have been a terrific collision at home plate." However, with the five-foot-nine, 160-pound Alou running, the Giants weren't willing to take that chance.

Universally respected sportswriter Red Smith, who was covering the game and therefore an eyewitness to the play, put the odds of Alou scoring on that play at "ten-to-one, against."

Yankees manager Ralph Houk, who was admittedly biased, declared, "Matty would have been out by a mile."

"It would have been suicide to send Matty home," chimed in San Francisco sportswriter Art Rosenbaum, who was also on the scene.

Lockman and the Giants did not want the World Series to end with the tying run thrown out at home plate while left-handed slugger Willie McCovey waited in the on-deck circle with Orlando Cepeda behind him. Even Jack Sanford had to agree with that strategy. It made baseball sense. During the season, McCovey and Cepeda had belted 55 home runs and driven in 198 runs between them. In the Series, however, the right-hand hitting Cepeda was batting an anemic .156.

But that debate would have to wait.

Now, with the game and the Series on the line, Terry, who topped the American League with 23 wins during the regular season, convinced Ralph Houk, who had succeeded Casey Stengel, to let him remain in the game to face McCovey. What's more, Terry told his manager he wanted to pitch to the left-hand hitting McCovey rather than walk him to load the bases and set up force plays all around—even though McCovey had tripled his previous at-bat and homered off Terry in Game Two.

"I don't know what the hell I'm doing out here," growled Houk, the gruff World War II army major who received the Bronze Star and the Silver Star for his role in the Battle of the Bulge. "You want to pitch to

McCovey or Cepeda?"

"I'd rather pitch to McCovey," Terry replied.

Houk, his mouth, as usual, packed with chewing tobacco, spat. "You're pitching the game," the Yankees manager replied. "Go ahead."

In his book, *100 Years of the World Series*, author Eric Enders called Houk's decision to let Terry pitch to McCovey "one of the worst strategic decisions in World Series history."

Jim Murray, writing in the *Los Angeles Times*, agreed. "Terry was the only one who wanted to pitch to McCovey," Murray wrote. "He was also the only one with the baseball."

With Alou on third and the speedy Mays at second, all that the Giants needed was a base hit to tie and probably win the game.

McCovey tore into Terry's first pitch but the wind pushed the ball foul as it sailed into the upper deck in right field.

Out near second base, the Yankees' Bobby Richardson, expecting Terry to throw a curve, moved a step to his left and readied himself for the next pitch.

"The thing I remember when McCovey came up, I was down in my position, ready, and the NL ump said, 'Hey, Rich, can I have your cap for my little cousin?' " Richardson recalled in a 2007 interview with the *New York Times*.

Terry threw a fastball high and inside and the loud crack of McCovey's bat against the ball told Terry, and everyone in both dugouts, that McCovey had crushed the ball. "I thought I had a hit," McCovey said later. But as Terry whirled around, he saw that Richardson had snagged the sinking line drive, shoulder high, for the final out.

"People often suggest that I was out of position on that play," recalled Richardson. "But McCovey hit two hard ground balls to me earlier in the Series, so I played where I thought he would hit the ball. I moved over just a little bit and he hit the ball right to me. It was one of those balls like Mantle used to hit, with a lot of overspin. It looked like a base hit going to the outfield, but it came down in a hurry. He hit it really hard."

In the Yankees dugout, the bench rose in unison. "When McCovey hit that ball every single player on the bench went up," said reserve Phil Linz. "When Bobby leaped, we all leaped. The whole bench. Everyone's feet were off the ground. We caught that ball, all of us."

Meanwhile, across the field, the Giants' hearts rose as one, then sank.

"It was an instant thing, a bam-bam type of play," Giants catcher Tom Haller recalled. "A bunch of us jumped up like, 'There it is!' then sat down because it was over. It was one of those split-second things: 'Yeah! No!' "

"That was twice as hard a line drive as any man can hit," manager Al Dark declared.

In the bedlam that followed, Richardson yanked off his cap and, true to his promise, handed it to the umpire. "The picture in *The Times* showed me running in to Ralph Terry, hatless," Richardson said. "And in the background you can see the umpire looking at the cap I gave him."

"I'm the luckiest man in the country," the elated Terry admitted afterwards. "This has to be the greatest game I have ever pitched."

That hero could have been Jack Sanford, accepting handshakes and hugs all around—if only McCovey had belted that ball a couple feet higher, or a couple feet to Richardson's right or left. But that was typical of the type of luck that had haunted Jack Sanford throughout his career. "I never pitched better in my life," Jack declared after Game Seven.

According to Giants catcher Tom Haller, nobody on the team questioned Lockman's decision to halt Alou at third. "That's what's so great about baseball," Haller said. "I've got a highlight film of that World Series. The way they edited that film, you would say it's a good thing Alou didn't get sent. But had you been given a full picture of the play looking from above, there might have been some second-guessing.

"We held our heads high after that," Haller added.

"Even though we didn't win the World Series, we played well, and we had hopes of winning a lot more pennants."

In his postgame press conference, Ralph Houk, who called it "the toughest game I have ever managed," suggested he and Terry had agreed to "pitch around" McCovey. However, as Jim Murray noted in his column the next morning, "Pitching around McCovey is about as simple as pitching around the Empire State Building."

After the game, according to noted baseball writer Arnold Hano, who was shadowing Sanford in pursuit of a story, Jack retreated to the trainer's room off the clubhouse and sat on one of the rubbing tables, his back slumped against the wall, silently brooding over an open can of beer. Normally, the trainer's room is off-limits to reporters. But on this sad day, the writers intruded. Apparently no one had the energy to throw them out. The Giants were all drained.

Third baseman Jim Davenport sat next to Jack, talking, without much enthusiasm, about playing golf the next day with Al Dark. Don Larsen sat in the corner. Three times he muttered the same four-letter obscenity, which need not be repeated here. Chuck Hiller came into the room and grumbled to nobody in particular, "The (bleeping) Yankees!"

For nearly a full hour Jack sat there, rarely moving, refusing to talk to the reporters. Instead, without looking up, he answered their inquiries with, "I do not want to answer questions." But the writers, realizing Jack was the story, persisted. Finally, Sanford whispered, "I lost. That's all. I just lost."

In the fifth inning, when the Yankees scored the game's only run, Sanford had walked opposing pitcher Ralph Terry.

"Were you missing with fastballs when you walked Terry?" a reporter inquired.

"Sure, I was," Jack snapped. "Hell, yes, I was. Why do you think I walked him?"

Finally, according to Arnold Hano, Sanford stood up and walked through the somber, silent Giants clubhouse and across the hall to the Yankees locker room, where he quietly congratulated Ralph Terry.

Outside the clubhouse, Jack's wife Patsy and six-year-old daughter Laura waited. "I remember meeting him outside the clubhouse afterwards and him being really, really shut down," Laura Sanford recalled. "Not in a great mood. But yet he was mobbed with people.

"He wasn't signing any autographs. So people were asking me for my autograph.

"It seemed like we had to walk quite a ways to get a taxi and the taxi was just covered with people," she continued. "People had their hands in the windows or were climbing on top of the cab. They were celebrating my dad but he was devastated. He did what he could. He pitched three games in the World Series. It's hard to do better than that. But my dad felt like that one bad day made him a complete failure."

Later, Jack would say, "I never realized how difficult it would be to take a World Series loss. It hurts, really hurts. But maybe I proved something against the Yankees. Except for the very few, nobody is going to overpower them, so I didn't try to."

As sportswriter Bill Libby wrote, "He came close to being the hero of the Series. Very close. He was the best of all the San Francisco Giants in the Series, but he was disappointed when it was over. It fit the pattern of his baseball life."

Although Jack Sanford and Ralph Terry would both later be overshadowed by teammates Juan Marichal and Whitey Ford, respectively, when it came time for Hall of Fame balloting, the 1962 World Series belonged to them. Sanford and Terry went head-to-head three times. Terry won two games, Sanford won one. Terry compiled an earned-run average of 1.80 in those three games. Jack's ERA was 1.93. Terry struck out 16 hitters in his three Series starts. Sanford fanned 19. But because of one play, Terry emerged a conquering hero, while Jack was so crushed he still couldn't bear to watch a replay of the game more than 30 years later.

Terry was voted the Series Most Valuable Player and, as his reward, drove home in a new Corvette. Jack went home with his head hanging. Had the Giants won the Series, the MVP Award would surely have gone to Jack.

Sanford won 24 games during the 1962 season and lost seven. Terry won 23 games while losing 12. Their careers were remarkably similar, too. Jack pitched in the big leagues for 12 years. He won one 137 games and lost 101. His lifetime earned-run average was 3.69. Terry also pitched in the big leagues for 12 years. He won 107 games and lost 99. His lifetime ERA was 3.62. Like Sanford, Terry turned to golf after he left baseball, playing in several PGA and Seniors tour events. In the end, all that separated the two men was that one play.

The seventh game of the 1962 World Series was a baseball gem, one of the best deciding games in the history of the Fall Classic—even if the way it ended was particularly painful for Sanford, the Giants, and their fans.

There are some numbers, some hallowed, some haunting, that are forever woven into the fabric of baseball: It is 60 feet, six inches from the pitcher's mound to home plate. It is 90 feet from home plate to first base. But for those men, including Jack Sanford, who were fortunate enough to reach the 1962 World Series wearing the flannels of the San Francisco Giants, "two feet" was a number that lived in infamy.

If only McCovey had lashed his two-out ninth-inning line drive two feet higher or a couple of feet to Richardson's right or left, the Giants would have been 1962 baseball champions of the world—and Jack Sanford would have been forever remembered as a postseason hero.

But Jack wasn't the only one who was haunted by that fateful final play. "I broke in with a four-for-four in my first game in my rookie year against a Hall of Fame pitcher, Robin Roberts," McCovey later lamented. "I hit more grand slams [18] than anybody in National League history. I hit more home runs [521] than any left-handed hitter in the National League. But that out is what many people remember about me.

"I would rather be remembered as the guy who hit the ball six inches over Bobby Richardson's head."

Easily overlooked in the dramatic wake of the World Series was the fact that Jack Sanford, the ace of the San Francisco pitching staff, actually outhit his Hall of Fame teammate, Willie Mays. Jack went three-for-seven (.429) against Yankee pitching in the 1962 Series while the nonpareil Mays, who admittedly was worn out after the elongated season, was seven-for-twenty-eight (.250). Mickey Mantle, the New York Yankees' superstar, matched Sanford with three hits in the '62 Series. But it took Mantle 25 turns at bat to get them.

Sanford made three starts in the 1962 World Series. Against a lineup that included Mantle, Maris, and Berra, Sanford struck out 19 Yankees and allowed just 16 hits in 23⅓ innings, compiling a most impressive 1.93 earned-run average. Against Sanford, Yankee sluggers Mantle,

Maris, and Berra managed just two hits in 20 at-bats, hitting a humble .100.

However, in Sanford's three starts, the Giants scored just eight runs on his behalf. "With those two lineups, everybody thought it was going to be 9–8 every day," Jack recalled years later. "But both teams ended up scoring hardly any runs at all."

For Jack's efforts during the regular season, he finished second behind the Los Angeles Dodgers' Don Drysdale in the balloting for the 1962 Cy Young Award, which then was presented to the best pitcher in Major League Baseball, not separately for the National and American Leagues. Drysdale, who won 25 games that year to Sanford's 24, and led the NL in strikeouts, received 14 votes from the sportswriters to Jack's four. Jack also finished seventh behind baseball's new stolen base king, the Dodgers' Maury Wills, in voting for the NL Most Valuable Player Award.

"Boy, what a year," Jack declared. "I was as surprised as anybody else at the year I had."

By then the country was consumed by talk of the Cuban Missile Crisis. Only Jack Sanford was still playing Game Seven of the World Series, over and over again, in his head.

BALL 0 STRIKE 2 OUT 2

FAIR-PLAY by TRANSLUX

	1	2	3	4	5	6	7	8	9	TOTAL
VISITOR	☐	☐	☐	☐	☐	☐	☐	☐	☐	☐
HOME	☐	☐	☐	☐	☐	☐	☐	☐	☐	☐

NO REGRETS. NONE WHATSOEVER

Jack Sanford pitched seven solid years for the San Francisco Giants, his most memorable season, of course, coming in 1962.

"When he was with the Giants, during the best times, I remember people sending gifts to all of us," Jack's daughter Laura recalled. "I remember huge flower arrangements being delivered. People wanted us kids to sample cereals and soft drinks, and provide our 'feedback.' Crazy stuff like that."

Following Sanford's singularly successful 1962 season, the board of selectmen who governed Wellesley, Massachusetts, honored the best baseball player the city had ever produced. February 7, 1963, was designated as "Jack Sanford Day" in Wellesley. The celebration included a luncheon with the Kiwanis Club, visits to schools, and a banquet featuring roast rump of beef at Babson College's Knight Auditorium.

An estimated 500 townspeople and sports celebrities, including Boston Red Sox future Hall of Famer Carl Yastrzemski and then-manager Johnny Pesky, and Massachusetts-born pitchers Wilbur Wood (Cambridge) and Bill Monbouquette (Medford), turned out to pay tribute to Wellesley's favorite son. Also in attendance were Sanford's high school coach, Hal Goodnough, the man who had declined to recommend Jack to the Braves, and Frank Seyboth, the scout who first spotted Jack and signed him to a minor league contract with the Phillies. By then, Seyboth had followed Jack to San Francisco and was working as a scout for the Giants.

A testimonial heralding Jack's accomplishments in life up until then proclaimed, in part: "[He] has set a living example not only for the youth of Wellesley, but for the entire nation—an example of a young man who never gave up, and by clean living, hard work, sacrifice, and desire, reached the top. Overall he's just a grand guy, and that's why we're here this evening."

Jack's alma mater, Wellesley High School, also agreed to honor the team's best pitcher each year with the "Jack Sanford Award," a tribute that was phased out over time.

In 1963, Jack led the National League with 42 starts and, for the fifth year in a row and the sixth time in his career, he worked more than 200 innings. Jack won 16 games that summer, losing 13—the seventh year in a row that he reached double digits in victories. Jack struck out 158 batters in '63—his best effort in that regard since he fanned 188 in his rookie season of 1957. What's more, he walked only 76 hitters in 284 innings. It was the heaviest workload of his career. What made Sanford's 1963 season all the more impressive was the fact that Jack was 34 years old.

"Jack was playing baseball when I was eight years old and my interest was beginning," recalled son-in-law Bill Blagg, who later played golf and went hunting and fishing with Jack. "Unfortunately, in those days, the only game you could watch on TV was the Saturday 'Game of the Week.' We never missed the game on Saturday. It was a spectacle. The game was always the New York Yankees and whomever they were playing. I knew about every Yankee player and some of them were my heroes.

"I talked to Jack when he was amenable to it, but all I knew about were the Yankee players," Blagg continued. "I asked him about Mantle, Maris, Berra, all of them. But he was so competitive, he never said anything good or bad about them. So I switched and asked him who the best hitter he ever faced was. Of course, it was somebody in the National League who I was not very familiar with.

I never talked about the World Series because I knew by then how sensitive he was about that.

"What my discussions with Jack about baseball revealed to me was how truly competitive he still was about his life and his career," said Blagg, who played baseball in college. "I always felt I was a highly competitive person in sports. And I was. However, Jack's will and competitive nature were at a far different level. He was so intense."

For example, Jack normally wore size 10 shoes. However, according to his son, John, "Throughout his baseball career he wore a size seven shoe on his right foot because he said he could 'push off' stronger with the smaller shoe. Years of this practice resulted in a deformed right foot and lots of problems later in life with the foot."

The numbness in Jack's fingers returned in 1964, marching up his right arm. "It was really a scary feeling," he recalled. "I couldn't do a thing. I couldn't cut the kids' meat. I couldn't use it. I'd go to do something naturally, pick something up, and it would just fall out of my hand." As a result, Sanford appeared in just 18 games in '64, winning five and losing seven. Jack's days as a full-time starting pitcher were over.

Doctors discovered that a blood clot had cut off Jack's circulation. In a 12-hour operation, surgeons removed the blood clot and transplanted a section of a vein from his right ankle into the artery under his armpit. "It's like a tire patch," Jack joked. "A 10,000-mile guarantee at least, I hope."

Seriously, Jack later acknowledged, "I was very thankful that I didn't lose my arm."

"It was very dicey—a twelve-and-a-half-hour surgery was kind of unheard-of," recalled Laura Sanford. "I remember my dad showing me his scar later and saying, 'The doctors said the blood clot just kept coming. They just kept pulling it out. It didn't stop.' That was a weird image in my mind."

In November 1964 Sanford went to the Arizona Instructional League to find out if he could still pitch. "The first time I started throwing I was scared to death," he admitted. But the repair job worked and Jack opened the 1965 season in the Giants' starting rotation.

On June 18 Sanford shut out the New York Mets for seven innings in a 3–0 win to run his record to 4–1. Jack started five more games for the Giants, but only lasted past the third inning once.

On August 18, the Giants sold him to the California Angels where Jack was reunited with his former manager, Bill Rigney. He appeared in nine games for the Angels in 1965, starting five and pitching the rest of the time in relief. Jack won one game with the Angels and lost two, bringing his season record to 5–7.

Rigney converted Sanford to a relief pitcher in 1966

and, temporarily anyway, revived his career. Jack appeared in 50 games in '66, pitching out of the bullpen in all but six, more often than not in middle relief. Although he only pitched 108 innings, Jack won 13 games and lost seven. That made him the Angels' winningest pitcher, along with veteran starter George Brunet, on a team that finished sixth in the 10-team American League. Jack, who also saved five games for the Angels, was even named on four sportswriters' Most Valuable Player ballots.

All things considered, it was a remarkable turnaround. Before games, Jack often found himself in the locker room, trading stories about the good old days with Angels owner Gene Autry, the Singing Cowboy, in his trademark white cowboy hat and bolo tie, along with other veteran players.

Nevertheless, Jack, the Angels' second-oldest pitcher at 37, wasn't happy. "Let's face it, the only reason a guy is in the bullpen is because he's not good enough to start," he grumbled.

"He was certainly on the downward side of his career," said daughter Laura. "He was aware of it. And he wasn't happy about it."

Sanford returned to the Angels' starting rotation in 1967. But on June 15, after nine starts, with Jack's record at 3–2 and an unsightly 4.47 ERA, the Angels traded him, along with Jackie Warner, to the Kansas City Athletics for Roger Repoz.

"I remember the summer that he was traded to the Kansas City A's," recalled Laura, who was 12 at the time. "We had rented this beautiful place for the summer in Yorba Linda, California, which is a really nice suburb of Anaheim. There were tons of kids. These kids were skateboarding and I had never really seen anybody skateboard before. That was so cool.

"Then my dad was traded. My parents were upset. Susan had been born, she was about seven months old. So my parents had four kids, including a baby, and we went to live in a hotel where all the 'homeless' ballplayers stayed in Kansas City for three weeks. We'd all go into the dining room to eat, including the baby, order lunch every day at the pool and hang out with the other players. It was crazy, crazy, crazy. Then we rented a house in Independence, Missouri. It was a very stressful time for both of my parents.

"My father's baseball career was waning and I think he knew his release was imminent," Laura added. "As he characterized himself, he was 'a has-been.' When dad eventually got a CB radio many years later, he gave himself the handle 'Has Been.' "

The trade reunited Jack with another of his former managers, Alvin Dark. Pitching out of the Athletics bullpen, Jack's ERA climbed to 5.12 and on August 15, Kansas City released him. Dark, who had convinced the

San Francisco Giants to keep Jack six years earlier when the front office wanted to discard him in the expansion draft, now tried to make him the Athletics' pitching coach. But Charlie Finley, the Athletics' iconoclastic, tight-fisted owner, said no. Although it was very disappointing at the time, that turned out to be a blessing in disguise.

Five days later, Dark himself was fired. Finley accused his manager of conspiring with the A's players who had drafted a letter critical of the often-overbearing owner. Dark and his coaching staff were fired, rehired, and then fired again, all in the middle of one night between 1:30 and 5:30 a.m.

"Dad took me to the ballpark the day he was released," John recalled. "We cleaned out his locker and he gave me his huge duffel bag to carry as he went around and said goodbye to all the players. I was about ten but had a good idea of what was going on. I thought he was going to be mad but actually he seemed relieved, ready to move on. I'll never forget that day."

After 137 major league wins and 101 losses, with a 3.69 earned-run average, Jack Sanford's pitching career was over. However, that career was far from ordinary. According to the *New York Times*, a 2007 survey showed that the average career of a player during what is sometimes referred to as baseball's Golden Age (1946–68) lasted 6.47 years. Jack survived in the major leagues for almost twice that long. In the majors, as in the minors, he persevered.

Years after Jack had retired from baseball, he admitted to author Mike Mandel that his early rejection at that Red Sox tryout camp and his prolonged, frustrating trek through the minor leagues were what had fueled the anger and anxiety that plagued him throughout his career. "Every day felt like a matter of survival, of just staying there," Sanford said. "I could never really relax and consider myself a major leaguer.

"But without baseball," Jack added, "I probably never would have enjoyed life as much as I have. I have no regrets, none whatsoever."

On the mound, Sanford was once described as looking like a bull. "He picks up the rosin bag and throws it down," wrote Bill Libby in his 1963 feature article about Jack in *Sport* magazine. "He scuffs around like a bull, tugging at his sleeves, kicking up small sandstorms with his toes, growling to himself, talking to the batters, holding the ball a half-minute at a time.

"His motion is clumsily powerful. He rears back, stretches his right arm low, kicks high, and fires. He used to be so off-balance at the end of these awkward explosions, he couldn't field his position."

Perhaps because it took Jack so long to get to the big leagues, perhaps because he had suffered so much along the way, or maybe because he had so little confidence in his own ability, he would cut himself off from the rest of the world before he pitched. Many starting pitchers retreat into a cocoon of unapproachability on the day they are scheduled to work. Jack, never a glib, gregarious sort, was no exception. He would stop speaking to everyone, including his wife and kids. And he would toss and turn. sleeplessly in bed the night before each start, constantly reviewing how he planned to pitch to each hitter.

In the clubhouse, on the days when he was scheduled to pitch, Jack would endlessly circle the room, according to Libby, "walking round and round, scowling at his teammates, without a word for them, resisting the slightest distraction. He is like a prisoner pacing his cell in the death house.

"Even after a game, even after a victory, he is tense and silent," continued Libby. "It is sometimes through the next day before he relaxes. And then he begins to look ahead to his next start."

When Jack disagreed with an umpire's call on one of his pitches, he would stomp around the mound, waving his arms and talking to himself. "I don't think he saw the catcher, batter, and umpire; I don't think he saw anything," recalled former catcher Hobie Landrith, who was Jack's occasional batterymate in San Francisco. "When he was out there, he was one bundle of nerves that couldn't wait to get the ball and throw it again. He never wanted the catcher even approaching him. He'd yell, 'Give me the ball! Give me the ball! GIVE ME THE BALL!' "

After a loss, according to Libby, Sanford would "throw up a wall of sullen silence and hide behind it." Many of the San Francisco baseball beat writers wouldn't even waste their time going to the Giants clubhouse in search of a comment from Sanford after he lost.

When asked about his relationship with the sportswriters, Jack once admitted, "They scare me."

On September 15, 1962, after Pittsburgh Pirates rookie third baseman Bob Bailey, a .143 hitter, tripled in the bottom of the eighth inning to drive in two runs and help end Sanford's historic 16-game winning streak, an intrepid reporter approached Jack and asked, "What kind of pitch did you throw Bailey?"

"What kind of pitch did you think it was?" Sanford snapped back.

"I thought it was a fastball," the writer said.

"Did you think it was a triple?" Jack snarled.

End of interview.

Once plagued by wildness, Sanford learned to better control his pitches and cut down on walks and therefore on base runners. "I'm more conscious of the need for economy on base runners," he explained. "They can't score if they don't get on."

Jack also learned to better control his temper. He still

got angry but he no longer came unglued at every bad pitch, base hit, or umpire's blown call.

Although he included a curveball, a slider, and a changeup in his repertoire, Sanford remained a very hard thrower, relying on his trademark fastball to get hitters out more often than not. "I have to put every ounce of strength into every fastball I throw or I get blasted," he explained. "I can't pace myself."

How hard did Jack throw? "We didn't have radar guns back then, so we didn't know what his top velocity was, but it was fast," recalled former Giants third baseman Jim Davenport, one of Jack's teammates in 1962. "He was a great competitor and we all enjoyed playing behind him."

~

After Sanford was released by the Kansas City Athletics in 1967 and Jack's benefactor, Al Dark, was fired, both men landed on their feet with the Cleveland Indians. In 1968, the Indians hired Dark to be their new manager and Dark quickly invited Jack to be his pitching coach. "Jack Sanford is one of my favorite people," Dark explained.

"Alvin Dark was Dad's best friend in baseball," remembered John Sanford. "They met in San Francisco when Dark was hired as the new manager and reunited in Cleveland when he hired Dad as the pitching coach. Alvin was a superb athlete, excelling in both football and baseball at LSU. Baseball experts said that Alvin was Hall of Fame material but for his time in the military during World War II. His success continued after his playing years as a manager; he is one of only a few managers to ever win pennants in both the National and American Leagues.

"Alvin was always calm and friendly when I was around him," John continued. "I looked up to him and knew that Dad had complete respect for the man. Ironically, Dad used to tell a story about a game the Giants blew in the ninth inning. When they got to the locker room, Alvin was so pissed off he picked up a metal stool and hurled it across the room. Unfortunately, his pinky finger got caught in the stool and it literally ripped off the end of his finger.

"Alvin's second wife had a son named Rusty who was my age. When we went to Cleveland, Rusty was there and we became fast friends. We were twelve years old and on road trips Alvin would room with my dad while Rusty and I got to stay in the manager's suite. Nothing better than being twelve and having the best room in a hotel full of MLB players, not to mention room service at three a.m.

"One night in Fenway we had front row behind home plate," John recalled. "When one of our guys hit a homer to go ahead, we started to climb up the safety netting. Stadium security pulled us off the netting and were escorting us out of the stadium. When they asked us where our parents were we told them one was in the dugout and the other in the bullpen. I'll never forget the look on those guys' faces! Soon we were back in our front row seats."

As the Indians' new manager, Dark wanted Sanford to work with Sam McDowell, a free-spirited young left-handed pitcher with a blazing fastball. McDowell himself later said Jack taught him to slow down and think on the mound. Sudden Sam won 15 games under Sanford's supervision in 1968 and led the American League in strikeouts with 283. The following season, McDowell won 18 games and struck out 279.

With Sanford as his pitching coach, Luis Tiant, who had a reputation for fading late in the season, won 21 games for the Indians in 1968 and led the AL with a career-best 1.60 ERA.

"Jack couldn't break a pane of glass the last several years that he pitched," McDowell recalled later, "but he knew how to pitch. There never has been a man in my career who helped me more. And I worked with Jack only two years. He had the unique quality of knowing me better than I knew myself. He pumped me up without me knowing it. He helped me have my best years."

According to Sanford, at the end of the 1969 season, when he informed Dark and the Indians that he was leaving baseball to work in golf full-time, "Sam McDowell offered me part of his 1970 raise if I changed my mind."

In McDowell's first start of the 1970 season, he slipped on the wet mound and couldn't finish the game. "That night, the first person who called me was Jack Sanford from West Palm Beach," McDowell said. "He wanted to know if I was all right."

While Jack was the Indians' pitching coach, his son, John, then 12 years old, frequently accompanied his dad to the ballpark for home games. "One day I had to get something out of the car for him before we left the house and somehow I broke the key off in the door lock," John recalled. "This, of course, required a locksmith and made us at least an hour late to the ballpark.

"Dad was pissed and told me I had to explain the reason for us being late to manager Alvin Dark. I was scared shitless. Dad was a stickler for being on time and was always the first guy there and the last to leave. After I told Alvin the story, he sternly told me that I owed him a dozen golf balls for making Dad late. This was a tall order since I had no money and no way to buy the new golf balls.

"After agonizing over this impossible request, I got the idea to go to the local driving range and paid fifty cents for a dozen old beat-up range balls. I knew that was not what Alvin wanted, but it was the best I could do.

"I put the old balls in a new box and when I handed them to Alvin I thought I would be scolded again," John continued. "But much to my surprise and amazement, he was impressed with my creativity and made a big joke about it. I guess it was the old-school way of teaching me the lesson of being on time."

After two seasons as the Indians' pitching coach, Jack left baseball to go to work full-time for the Perini family, who were building and operating golf courses in Florida. At age 40, Jack Sanford embarked on his second career.

> "Ralph Terry gets set. Here's the pitch to Willie.
> There's a liner straight to Richardson!
> The ballgame is over and the World Series is over!"
>
> — George Kell, calling the last out of Game 7 on NBC Radio.

BETTER A HAS-BEEN
THAN A NEVER-WAS

When Jack Sanford left baseball, after a career that had spanned 22 years in the major and minor leagues as a player and, briefly, as a coach, he went to work for the family of his childhood friend, Lou Perini Jr., and the Perini Land and Development Company. Many professional athletes struggle to make the transition to their second and sometimes third careers. Many never find the success and happiness they had known in sports. Once again, Jack proved to be an exception.

Sanford, who had loved to play with a toy golf club and ball when he was a toddler, rediscovered the game in 1962 after he suffered that crushing defeat in the seventh and deciding game of the World Series. Knowing that

Jack was distraught and despondent about the Series loss, San Francisco Giants manager Al Dark, himself an avid golfer, bought Jack a set of clubs that fall, hoping the new game might help take his pitcher's mind off the dramatic Game Seven defeat. Sanford, fiercely competitive and a fine athlete, began hitting balls and soon became consumed by the game. He practiced constantly and, like many baseball pitchers, took advantage of his days off between starts to play golf as often as he could during the season. Within a few years, he was down to a three-handicap.

"If I had my choice, I definitely would have played golf rather than try baseball," Jack told a reporter in a 1972 interview.

After Sanford finished second behind Ken Harrelson in a baseball players' golf tournament, he mused about trying his hand on a professional golf tour. "If I had ten years back, I'd really think about it," Jack said. "[Baseball] was a tough job for me. I didn't have that much ability," added Jack, self-effacing as always.

Ironically, according to brother-in-law Phil Reynolds, Jack considered golf "a sissy sport" until Dark gave him that set of clubs. "The rascal took up golf on the West Coast and he went flying by me," Reynolds said.

In 1964, Jack and his wife Pat, now with three kids, had begun thinking about life after baseball. Once again, the Perini connection came into play. The Perini family had spent years buying up undeveloped land in Florida. They owned some 5,000 acres in the West Palm Beach area and were planning, among other things, to build a golf course.

By this time, Jack's golf game had improved to the point where he could seriously begin looking at the golf business as a possible second career. Jack contacted the Perinis, who offered him a position as "Sports Representative." Jack's job, basically, would be to play golf with local dignitaries and investors, tell a few baseball stories, and invite his former teammates and major league friends to play golf at the resort and thus impress the members.

In the winter of 1965, Jack and his family moved to West Palm Beach, Florida.

Pat, Susan, Nancy, Jack, and John

"The summer that we were living in Independence, Missouri, when my dad was playing for the Kansas City Athletics [1967], we belonged to a country club," recalled daughter Laura. "Us kids were all on the swim team and there were swim meets. It was really fun. And my dad was playing golf. And he was loving golf.

"It was about at that point that the Perini Corporation

hired him to do some public relations work," she continued. "He'd come and speak at different meetings. He was kind of a draw because of his sports background. And he liked doing it.

"They offered him a job running a golf course in West Palm Beach. You know, 'Come and play golf with Jack Sanford.'

"He wasn't just a personality," Laura said. "He opened the place, he closed the place, and he directed the grounds crew. He did all the hard work. But he loved the golf game, and people liked to play with Jack Sanford, or hang out with him—people from Massachusetts who were friends of the Perinis, snowbirds from Massachusetts and Connecticut wanted to come down, buy a condo there, become members."

Sanford worked first at the Palm Beach Lakes Golf Center and later as director of golf at the President Country Club and Bear Lakes Country Club in West Palm Beach, Florida. Meanwhile, he continued to scout part-time for the Cleveland Indians into the 1980s.

"Jack became a great golfer," said friend and frequent playing partner Jeff DeCiccio. "But he was so competitive. He would beat himself up if he missed a putt or hooked a drive. When that happened, he would get real quiet—too damn serious.

"When I was his partner, he would give me hell. He'd say, 'Jeffrey, concentrate on what you're doing!' And these were only two-dollar bets. If you had a bad day, you could lose ten dollars. But for Jack, it was not about the money. It was about the competition and the bragging rights."

On the golf course, as on the baseball diamond, Jack's temper was often his trademark. "It has been noted that John had quite a temper and it showed up quite often on the golf course," recalled Phil Reynolds. "He once hit a six-iron poorly and he threw that six-iron farther than I can hit a six-iron. Most of the time though, around me, he did keep his temper in check."

"Dad had a legendary temper on the golf course," admitted John, who became his dad's frequent playing partner. "What helped him at times on the mound did not bode well on the course.

"By this time he was a scratch golfer, but his wild displays of anger on the course are what define his golf personality to this day. When I run into the old-timers who played golf with him they always have a story about one of his tantrums on the course.

"One time, he was playing a match at the old Palm Beach Lakes Golf Course which Perini had built and where Dad was the manager. It must have been a fairly serious match and when he missed a short putt on eighteen to lose the match, he threw his putter, then crossed his arms in front of him, put his left hand in his right front pocket and his right hand in his left front pocket and literally tore his pants off!

"I must add that the same old-timers that tell the many stories of Dad's on-course antics also talk about how much they loved him and his competitive spirit," John continued.

"Naturally I grew up playing golf with Dad and always had mixed feelings when on the course. I loved being with him and we played in many father-son tourneys but the pressure was tremendous and therefore we probably underachieved most of the time.

"That said," he added, "I have great memories of our rounds together and would not trade those days for anything."

As for the Sanford family's home life during the West Palm Beach days, Jack's daughter Nancy recalled: "Without the grueling baseball schedule, my dad was living at home year-round, but worked at the course and played golf almost every day of the week. My dad always worked long days, weekends, and holidays, including Christmas Day and Easter Sunday, leaving my mom at home with four kids.

"Most times, he would come home at night, have a few cocktails, eat dinner, watch TV, and go to bed. My mom would make sure there was a balanced dinner with dessert every night.

"The minute my dad came home from work, I could tell whether it was going to be a happy night on the Sanford home front. If my dad had a decent round of golf that day, he would be in a great mood, giving my mom a kiss on the cheek and asking us how our day went. If it was a bad day on the golf course, everyone would feel the tension in the air.

"When I was about ten years old, my dad taught me how to make his drink of choice and I would make him a gin and tonic with a twist of lime every night," Nancy continued. "My mom would join him outside on the patio or backyard with crackers and cheese, sardines, or some kind of appetizer.

"I usually made my dad several gin and tonics while my mom would enjoy one vodka and tonic. We had a pool, which was a luxury to us. As I reflect on this time period, I have fond memories—except when my dad was in a bad mood. On these occasions, he would become mean and derogatory toward my mom. An explosive argument usually followed and then several days of silence between my parents. This was extremely upsetting and stressful to me because I wanted my parents to get along and I despised confrontation.

"I remember my parents having a very tumultuous relationship. The good times were great and the bad times were very scary and intimidating. My mom was a stay-at-home mom for most of their marriage, so of course, she relied on my dad's paycheck and would rather try and keep the peace than get involved in an argument or even consider divorce.

"My dad was fairly strict with his kids—when he was home, he was the disciplinarian," recalled Nancy. "My brother and I knew what a leather belt felt like across the legs and butt when we acted up.

"My dad also knew how to have fun with us and occasionally took us fishing, swimming, and to the park. Once, I recall my parents took us shopping and we each picked out one big toy. This was a special day that I will always fondly remember."

Jack with Susan, Laura, and Nancy

Although Jack was never a good student himself, he made his kids' education a high priority. "He instilled in us the importance of achieving excellent grades in school and attending college," continued Nancy. "Although my parents did not have a lot of money back then, they managed to create college savings accounts for all of us. I do not recall my dad attending many of my school functions, but he did ask me about my grades and he placed significant importance on receiving all A's and B's on our report cards.

"I participated in sports throughout my childhood and like most kids, I always wanted to make my dad proud. I remember playing basketball in middle school and spraining my ankle. After it was healed and I could play on it, my dad would always tape it for me before games. These memorable moments of fatherly love were huge for me."

~

Back in the fall of 1961, the San Francisco Giants front office had decided to expose Jack to the expansion draft, until manager Al Dark talked the brass into hanging on to him. Had it not been for Dark, Jack might have been one of the much-ridiculed original Mets who lost 120 games in 1962—instead of starring in the World Series for the San Francisco Giants. But 10 years later, retired from baseball, Sanford found himself on the scene of one of the most tragic moments in Mets history.

When baseball's major league players went on strike at the end of spring training in 1972, suddenly shutting the game down, the New York Yankees and New York

Mets chartered a plane to fly their managers, coaches, and front office executives along with their families from Florida back to New York on Monday, April 3. Mets manager Gil Hodges and his coaching staff decided to spend the weekend at the Mets' team hotel in West Palm Beach, playing golf and relaxing.

Sunday, April 2, was Easter Sunday and, after playing 18 holes at the Palm Beach Lakes course, where old friend Jack Sanford happened to be the director of golf, Hodges excused himself, saying he wanted to make arrangements to have some fruit shipped home. He returned 15 minutes later and the foursome of Hodges, plus coaches Joe Pignatano, Rube Walker, and Eddie Yost, teed off for nine more holes.

After they finished playing, they returned to the clubhouse to have a few cold drinks with their buddy Jack Sanford. "Gilly, Piggy, Rube, and me shot the bull with Jack for a while," Eddie Yost recalled.

On their way back to the hotel, which was located next to the golf course, Pignatano asked, "What time should we meet for dinner?"

"Seven-thirty," Hodges replied.

Those were the last words the popular former Brooklyn Dodgers first baseman ever uttered.

According to Joe Pignatano, he had turned his back and was walking toward his hotel room when he heard Hodges's golf clubs hitting the walkway. When

Pignatano turned, he saw Hodges sprawled on the ground, blood gushing from a cut on his head. Hodges was rushed to a nearby hospital where he was pronounced dead of a heart attack, two days before his 48th birthday.

Earlier in the day, Mets pitcher Jerry Koosman, who was also staying at the hotel, had asked the coaches if one of them could warm him up, even though the players were on strike. "It was my day to throw on the side," explained Koosman, who, like the rest of major league baseball's players, had not yet come to grips with the fact that they were on strike.

"Rube [Walker] said, 'We're not allowed to do anything with the players because of the strike.' Rube said, 'Go get a catcher's mitt off the truck and some balls and go throw against the back wall of the hotel. Get your workout in.' "

Along the way, Koosman bumped into Minnesota Vikings football player Mick Tingelhoff in the lobby of the hotel. Tingelhoff, a future National Football League Hall of Famer, offered to warm the pitcher up. "He came back behind the hotel and a block away we could see Jack Sanford," Koosman recalled. "I started throwing and the looser I got, the more trouble Tingelhoff had catching me. I was hitting him in the chest and the knees. Finally, Jack felt sorry for him. He came over and took the glove away from him and he finished warming me up." Of course, neither Koosman nor Sanford had any inkling of the tragedy that would follow a short while later.

Over the years, the guys Jack met on the golf course, in Florida and in New England, would have loved to have heard Jack's many tales from his baseball days. But Jack was always reluctant to share. "He never really seemed to want to talk about baseball," recalled friend Jeff DeCiccio. "Now and then he would mention a name like Willie Mays or Mickey Mantle, but no long reports about his exciting life in baseball.

"He came one year as my guest to a business meeting in Arizona," continued DeCiccio, a senior vice president at UBS Financial Services in Worcester, Massachusetts. "I learned the Chicago Cubs were having spring training just up the road and I said to Jack, 'Why don't we go to a game?' Reluctantly, he said yes because he could see his old friend Don Zimmer. We went to the game, but Jack's heart wasn't in it and we left after four innings."

As son John remembered, "After Dad retired he didn't talk about baseball very much, but I was playing in Little League and every once in a while I would talk him into watching a game with me on TV. Once he got into the game he would predict every move the managers and coaches would make. He could tell what pitch was coming next, you know, curveball, slider, changeup, fastball, and he was right nine out of ten times. I learned a lot about baseball strategy just listening to him. He didn't come to many of my games but every now and then I would see him pull up to the field and watch from his truck. One time I pitched a no-hitter and when I got home that night he said, "Hey kid, good game tonight." He didn't hand out many attaboys; that meant the world to me."

With Jack's baseball days behind him, he shifted his energy to hobbies he felt passionate about, such as hunting and fishing. On one of his New England hunting trips with DeCiccio and his boss in the golf business, Joe Perini, he met former Detroit Tigers pitching sensation Mark "The Bird" Fidrych, who had captured the attention of the entire country in 1976. Both men were from the Boston area, both had been Rookie of the Year, and both enjoyed hunting. So it was not surprising that, despite the difference in their ages, they hit it off. Living in Florida, however, Jack had eventually acquired a bit of a southern accent. "We had lots of fun, kidding him about his redneck New England accent," DeCiccio said.

"My dad was a real sportsman," Laura said. "He was a big hunter. He would go hunting deer and he would hang the deer he shot from a tree in the yard." Back in the offseason days when he was with the Giants, Laura remembered, "My dad would go boar hunting. And I'd say, 'Boar? What's boar?' And he would describe the boar to me. We always ate what he killed. Rabbit and venison, pheasant and elk and boar. My mother would make boar burgers and elk steaks.

"My dad had this way with animals," Laura added, "whether it was an alligator, a cat, a bird, or a ferocious German shepherd. It was magical. The fiercest German shepherd would lick his face. He could talk down a monster."

"I used to have this little parrot when we lived in Florida," said daughter Nancy. "The parrot was allowed out of the cage a lot. The bird would sit on my father's shoulder and peel the sunburned skin off the tops of my dad's ears and drink out of his cocktail."

"Dad had a great love and respect for wildlife," agreed son John. While Jack was working as the director of golf at the President Country Club in West Palm Beach, Florida, he discovered a baby alligator in the lake on the 11th hole of the golf course and began feeding it. "Dad used to bring leftovers from the kitchen out to feed the gator," John Sanford recalled. "It didn't take long before he could whistle and the gator would come swimming toward us, looking for his next meal.

"This went on for several years and, of course, the gator got huge," John continued. "Folklore has it that once the reptile got plump enough and potentially dangerous to golfers, Dad showed up one rainy morning with his .38 and the rest is history. I'm sure the maintenance crew had a good meal that day."

~

In 1976, Jack suffered a heart attack.

"I remember my dad was sent up to Massachusetts General Hospital for open heart surgery," recalled Laura. "I was working on Martha's Vineyard that summer and I went to see him at the hospital.

"He made me go to the liquor store and get him gin and tonic and lime. The doctors had put him on a low-fat diet and he wanted a roast beef sandwich with cheese and mayonnaise. He thought it was hilarious. I didn't want to ruin his good time so I went along with it."

Jack and Pat, who had been separated, got back together during Jack's recuperation. "She nursed him back to health," Laura said.

But they divorced in 1979 and Pat Sanford moved back to Massachusetts.

"When my parents decided to separate, I was devastated," said Nancy. "I often wondered why I felt that way, living in such a pressure cooker atmosphere. I guess divorce was unacceptable at the time and I never wanted to see my parents split up.

"They eventually divorced and in the summer of 1979, my mom, sister Susan, and I moved back to Massachusetts. I also left for college that fall and only saw my dad once or twice a year for the next four years."

"My theory has always been that while Dad was in baseball, he was gone about half of the time," said son John. "When he retired, he was home full-time which had never happened before. Between the additional time at home and his transition out of the limelight—as Dad always put it, 'I'm a has-been'—there was a lot stress on my parents' relationship. And let's not forget the old 'midlife crisis.' "

According to John, "The divorce was messy and Dad never spoke to Mom afterwards. That was stressful for all of us." However, according to Laura, the divorced couple did dance together at John's wedding.

"Naturally, I think my mother was a saint and for the most part she was," John added. "To my knowledge, she never had another relationship after they split up."

Patricia Sanford passed away in 2013.

Jack remarried twice and eventually moved to Beckley, West Virginia.

"He loved those summers in West Virginia where he could shoot guns in the morning and play golf in the afternoon," said Jack's good friend Jeff DeCiccio. "It was the best of both worlds for Jack: Florida in the winter, playing golf and quail hunting; summer in Beckley; and two weeks with me, hunting in New England."

"I believe the last three or four years of his life were the happiest," said son John. "He was in a good marriage, all four kids had graduated from college and were doing well. He finally began to relax a little and enjoy the fruits of his lifelong labor."

Laura also recalled how content Jack was in Beckley: "His baseball memorabilia were on the wall and he still wore his World Series ring, but he was very much in the moment, be it playing with his granddaughter, or hunting or fishing in the pond. He gave all his attention to the people he was with."

Jack was often found on his porch relaxing and enjoying the hummingbirds eating from a feeder he filled with a special mix. During summer evening conversations he'd help guests spot hidden wildlife in the thickets. But Jack's competitive spirit was never too far away.

Jack had invited his son-in-law Bill Blagg to play many rounds of golf in the past, so when he invited him to play a tournament in Beckley, Bill didn't consider it had any special significance.

"I didn't know anything about how big the tournament was to folks in the area or to Jack," Bill said. Jack had tagged Bill to be his partner in the annual Glade Springs Member-Guest Tournament. After Jack had shot his age of 67 in the regular round, while team scores were being tallied, Bill popped a Miller Light, thinking the game was over. Jack approached and said, "Bill, I don't want you drinking until the end of the tournament. We're in the playoffs."

Jack and Bill and three other teams started the shootout followed by a crowd of more than 200 people, including Bill's wife, Nancy, their daughter Danielle, and many of Jack's friends who were all captivated by the thrilling spectacle. Bill recalled, "The atmosphere was like an old-time tournament with people following on foot and in golf carts. I was very nervous and couldn't hit the first drive. Jack was very calm, and took the shot instead. A lot of my golf partners are always giving me advice on rounds, but Jack wasn't like that. There was no pressure. He said, 'Billy, just play your game.' "

After a tense couple of holes, Jack made a two-foot putt to win the playoff and the tournament.

Jack, granddaughter Danielle, and Bill Blagg

"It was the most exciting thing I've ever done in golf," said Bill, "and to be invited by Jack was an honor. I loved Jack. He's the most competitive person I've ever met in my life, and to be with him when he was competing like that was unbelievable. He was so focused on winning the tournament."

Jack replayed the game shot by shot to the family members who hadn't been able to attend, bragging profusely about how well Bill had played. In Bill's version, he'd accidentally hit a few good shots, but Jack had carried him.

According to John, Jack considered that win the highlight of his golfing career. Jack continued to play regularly and enjoy his time at Glade Springs, until John noticed some concerning behavior.

"One day we were playing golf and I could tell his motor skills were off a bit," said John. "I forced him to get checked out and we found out he had a brain tumor. All those years of baseball, golf, hunting, and fishing with no sunblock had caught up to him. Melanoma had metastasized in his brain. Within four months he was gone."

Jack died on March 7, 2000, at age 70. At Jack's request, his ashes were laid to rest in Cape Cod Bay, where he had spent so many hours late in life, fishing for bluefish and striped bass. "Jack loved the Cape," DeCiccio said.

"We visited Jack two months before he died," continued DeCiccio. "He was in the fight of his life against brain cancer. One day, a friend called and asked, 'What's doing, Jack?' Jack replied, 'I'm just sitting here, waiting for the inevitable.' Typical Jack: short and to the point.

"At Jack's funeral in Beckley, one of his golfing buddies told a story Jack had told him about pitching against one of his former roommates, who happened to be pitching for the opposing team that day," DeCiccio continued. "The old roomie had hit the Giants' Willie Mays with a pitch and when the pitcher came up to bat Jack got the signal from the bench to hit him with the next pitch. So Jack hit him. Later in the game, the opposing pitcher, Jack's old roommate, came up to bat again. And Jack got the sign from the dugout: Hit him again. At that point, when Jack was originally telling the story, someone asked him, 'So what did you do?' To which Jack replied, 'I hit him again. I wasn't going back to the minors in the morning.' "

When Jack passed, the *New York Times* left Game Seven of the World Series out of the lead paragraph of Jack's obituary, which read: "Jack Sanford, a hard-throwing right-hander who won 16 consecutive games in propelling the San Francisco Giants to the 1962 National League pennant, died last Tuesday at a hospital in Beckley, W.Va. He was 70."

Game Seven of the 1962 World Series and Willie McCovey's crushing line drive were not mentioned until the 10th paragraph of the obit.

Perhaps, in death, Jack Sanford finally found peace.

Jack's Stats

Glossary

Year—A star indicates an All-Star that season.
A ring indicates the player appeared in WS for winning team.
Age—Player's age at midnight of June 30th of that year.

Lg—League
AL—American League (1901–present)
NL—National League (1876–present)
AA—American Association (1882–1891)
UA—Union Association (1884)
PL—Players League (1890)
FL—Federal League (1914–1915)
NA—National Association (1871–1875)

W—Wins

L—Losses

W-L%—Win-Loss Percentage
W / (W + L)
For players, leaders need one decision for every 10 team games.
For managers, minimum to qualify for leading is 320 games.

ERA—9 * ER / IP
For recent years, leaders need 1 IP per team game played.
Bold indicates lowest ERA using current stats.
Gold means awarded ERA title at end of year.

G—Games Played or Pitched

GS—Games Started

GF—Games Finished

CG—Complete Game

SHO—Shutouts
No runs allowed and a complete game.

SV—Saves

IP—Innings Pitched

H—Hits/Hits Allowed

R—Runs Scored/Allowed

ER—Earned Runs Allowed

HR—Home Runs Hit/Allowed

BB—Bases on Balls/Walks

IBB—Intentional Bases on Balls
First tracked in 1955.

SO—Strikeouts

HBP—Times Hit by a Pitch.

BK—Balks

WP—Wild Pitches

BF—Batters Faced

ERA+
100*[lgERA/ERA]
Adjusted to the player's ballpark(s).

FIP—Fielding Independent Pitching
This stat measures a pitcher's effectiveness at preventing HR, BB, HBP, and causing SO.

(13*HR + 3*(BB+HBP) - 2*SO)/IP + Constant$_{lg}$
The constant is set so that each season MLB average FIP is the same as the MLB avg ERA.

WHIP—(BB + H)/IP
For recent years, leaders need 1 IP per team game played.

H9—9 x H / IP
For recent years, leaders need 1 IP per team game played.

HR9—9 x HR / IP
For recent years, leaders need 1 IP per team game played.

BB9—9 x BB / IP
For recent years, leaders need 1 IP per team game played.

SO9—9 x SO / IP
For recent years, leaders need 1 IP per team game played.

SO/W—SO/W or SO/BB
For recent years, pitching leaders need 1 IP per team game played.
No batting leaders computed.

Awards—Summary of how player did in awards voting that year.
GG—Gold Glove
SS—Silver Slugger
MVP—Most Valuable Player
CYA—Cy Young Award
ROY—Rookie of the Year

Sanford's Complete Major League Record

Year	Age	Tm	Lg	W	L	W-L%	ERA	G	GS	GF	CG	SHO	SV	IP	H	R	ER	HR
1956	27	PHI	NL	1	0		1	1.4	3	1	1	0	0	0	13	7	2	2	0
1957 ★	28	PHI	NL	19	8	0.7	3.1	33	33	0	15	3	0	236.2	194	94	81	22
1958	29	PHI	NL	10	13	0.44	4.4	38	27	4	7	2	0	186.1	197	103	92	15
1959	30	SFG	NL	15	12	0.56	3.2	36	31	2	10	0	1	222.1	198	90	78	22
1960	31	SFG	NL	12	14	0.46	3.8	37	34	2	11	6	0	219	199	111	93	11
1961	32	SFG	NL	13	9	0.59	4.2	38	33	1	6	0	0	217.1	203	114	102	22
1962	33	SFG	NL	24	7	0.77	3.4	39	38	1	13	2	0	265.1	233	110	101	23
1963	34	SFG	NL	16	13	0.55	3.5	42	42	0	11	0	0	284.1	273	123	111	21
1964	35	SFG	NL	5	7	0.42	3.3	18	17	1	3	1	0	106.1	91	44	39	7
1965	36	TOT	MLB	5	7	0.42	4.1	32	21	6	0	0	3	120.1	127	66	55	13
1965	36	SFG	NL	4	5	0.44	4	23	16	4	0	0	2	91	92	50	40	11
1965	36	CAL	AL	1	2	0.33	4.6	9	5	2	0	0	1	29.1	35	16	15	2
1966	37	CAL	AL	13	7	0.65	3.8	50	6	19	0	0	5	108	108	51	46	11
1967	38	TOT	AL	4	4	0.5	5.1	22	10	5	0	0	1	70.1	77	44	40	7
1967	38	CAL	AL	3	2	0.6	4.5	12	9	2	0	0	1	48.1	53	26	24	6
1967	38	KCA	AL	1	2	0.33	6.6	10	1	3	0	0	0	22	24	18	16	1
12 Yrs				137	101	0.58	3.7	388	293	42	76	14	11	2049	1907	952	840	174
162 Game Avg.				14	10	0.58	3.7	39	29	4	8	1	1	205	190	95	84	17
SFG (7 yrs)				89	67	0.57	3.6	233	211	11	54	9	4	1405	1289	642	564	117
PHI (3 yrs)				30	21	0.59	3.6	74	61	5	22	5	0	436	398	199	175	37
CAL (3 yrs)				17	11	0.61	4.1	71	20	23	0	0	7	185.2	196	93	85	19
KCA (1 yr)				1	2	0.33	6.6	10	1	3	0	0	0	22	24	18	16	1
NL (10 yrs)				119	88	0.58	3.6	307	272	16	76	14	4	1841	1687	841	739	154
AL (3 yrs)				18	13	0.58	4.4	81	21	26	0	0	7	207.2	220	111	101	20

Year	Age	Tm	Lg	BB	IBB	SO	HBP	BK	WP	BF	ERA+	FIP	WHIP	H9	HR9	BB9	SO9	SO/W	Awards
1956	27	PHI	NL	13	0	6	1	0	0	54	275	4.7	1.54	4.8	0	9	4.2	0.46	
1957 ★	28	PHI	NL	94	2	*188*	3	1	12	989	124	3.3	1.22	7.4	0.8	3.6	7.1	2	AS,MVP-10,RoY-1
1958	29	PHI	NL	81	6	106	3	0	3	819	90	3.7	1.49	9.5	0.7	3.9	5.1	1.31	
1959	30	SFG	NL	70	4	132	7	2	7	933	120	3.7	1.21	8	0.9	2.8	5.3	1.89	
1960	31	SFG	NL	99	6	125	2	3	15	940	92	3.4	1.36	8.2	0.5	4.1	5.1	1.26	
1961	32	SFG	NL	87	7	112	5	4	3	923	90	4.1	1.33	8.4	0.9	3.6	4.6	1.29	
1962	33	SFG	NL	92	4	147	3	2	4	1100	112	3.7	1.23	7.9	0.8	3.1	5	1.6	CYA-2,MVP-7
1963	34	SFG	NL	76	8	158	5	4	4	1184	91	3.2	1.23	8.6	0.7	2.4	5	2.08	
1964	35	SFG	NL	37	8	64	4	1	1	447	108	3.4	1.2	7.7	0.6	3.1	5.4	1.73	
1965	36	TOT	MLB	40	8	56	7	2	6	525	87	4.2	1.39	9.5	1	3	4.2	1.4	
1965	36	SFG	NL	30	7	43	7	1	4	402	92	4.4	1.34	9.1	1.1	3	4.3	1.43	
1965	36	CAL	AL	10	1	13	0	1	2	123	74	3.5	1.53	10.7	0.6	3.1	4	1.3	
1966	37	CAL	AL	27	6	54	4	1	3	447	87	3.7	1.25	9	0.9	2.3	4.5	2	MVP-21
1967	38	TOT	AL	21	5	34	2	1	1	298	62	3.9	1.39	9.9	0.9	2.7	4.4	1.62	
1967	38	CAL	AL	7	1	21	0	1	0	196	70	3.7	1.24	9.9	1.1	1.3	3.9	3	
1967	38	KCA	AL	14	4	13	2	0	1	102	50	4.1	1.73	9.8	0.4	5.7	5.3	0.93	
12 Yrs				737	59	1182	46	21	59	8659	99	3.6	1.29	8.4	0.8	3.2	5.2	1.6	
162 Game Avg.				74	6	118	5	2	6	865	99	3.6	1.29	8.4	0.8	3.2	5.2	1.6	
SFG (7 yrs)				491	39	781	33	17	38	5929	100	3.6	1.27	8.3	0.7	3.1	5	1.59	
PHI (3 yrs)				188	8	300	7	1	15	1862	108	3.5	1.34	8.2	0.8	3.9	6.2	1.6	
CAL (3 yrs)				44	8	88	4	3	5	766	80	3.7	1.29	9.5	0.9	2.1	4.3	2	
KCA (1 yr)				14	4	13	2	0	1	102	50	4.1	1.73	9.8	0.4	5.7	5.3	0.93	
NL (10 yrs)				679	47	1081	40	18	53	7791	102	3.6	1.29	8.2	0.8	3.3	5.3	1.59	
AL (3 yrs)				58	12	101	6	3	6	858	75	3.8	1.34	9.5	0.9	2.5	4.4	1.74	

Source: http://www.baseball-reference.com/players/s/sanfoja02.shtml?redir

Sanford's 1962 World Series Box Scores of
Games 1, 5, and 7, Which Jack Started

Game 1 /

Thursday, October 4, 1962 at Candlestick Park (San Francisco Giants)

	1	2	3	4	5	6	7	8	9	R	H	E
New York Yankees	2	0	0	0	0	0	1	2	1	6	11	0
San Francisco Giants	0	1	1	0	0	0	0	0	0	2	10	0

PITCHERS: NYY - Ford
          SFG - O'Dell, Larsen (8), Miller (9)

          WP - Whitey Ford
          LP - Billy O'Dell
        SAVE - none

HOME RUNS: NYY - Boyer
           SFG - none

ATTENDANCE: 43,852

Game 5 /

Wednesday, October 10, 1962 at Yankee Stadium I (New York Yankees)

	1	2	3	4	5	6	7	8	9	R	H	E
San Francisco Giants	0	0	1	0	1	0	0	0	1	3	8	2
New York Yankees	0	0	0	1	0	1	0	3	x	5	6	0

PITCHERS: SFG - Sanford, Miller (8)
          NYY - Terry

          WP - Ralph Terry
          LP - Jack Sanford
        SAVE - none

HOME RUNS: SFG - Pagan
           NYY - Tresh

ATTENDANCE: 63,165

Stats

Game 7 /

Tuesday, October 16, 1962 at Candlestick Park (San Francisco Giants)

	1	2	3	4	5	6	7	8	9	R	H	E
New York Yankees	0	0	0	0	1	0	0	0	0	1	7	0
San Francisco Giants	0	0	0	0	0	0	0	0	0	0	4	1

PITCHERS: NYY - Terry
          SFG - Sanford, O'Dell (8)

          WP - Ralph Terry
          LP - Jack Sanford
          SAVE - none

HOME RUNS: NYY - none
           SFG - none

ATTENDANCE: 43,948

Source: http://www.baseball-reference.com/postseason/1962_WS.shtml

Sanford's 1957 All-Star Game Box Score

Pitching	IP	H	R	ER	BB	SO	HR	ERA	BF	GSc	IR	IS	WPA	aLI	RE24
Curt Simmons, L (0-1)	1	2	2	2	2	0	0	18	7	39			-0.207	1.15	-2.3
Lew Burdette	4	2	0	0	1	0	0	0	15		3	1	0.205	1.09	2.8
Jack Sanford	1	2	1	1	0	0	0	9	5		0	0	-0.06	0.69	-0.5
Larry Jackson	2	1	0	0	1	0	0	0	8		0	0	0.071	0.97	1
Clem Labine	1	3	3	1	0	1	0	9	7		0	0	-0.143	0.63	-2.5
Team Totals	**9**	**10**	**6**		**4**	**1**	**0**	**0**	**42**	**39**	**3**	**1**	**-0.134**	**0**	**-1.6**

C Simmons faced 4 batters in the 2nd inning.

Balks: None.

WP: B Pierce (1); J Sanford (1).

HBP: None.

IBB: None.

Source: http://www.baseball-reference.com/allstar/1957-allstar-game.shtmlredir

Sanford's Minor League Record

Year	Age	AgeDif	Tm	Lg	Lev	Aff	W	L	W-L%	ERA	RAvg	G	GS	GF	CG	SHO	SV	IP	H	R	ER
1948	19		2 Teams	2 Lgs	D	PHI	3	15	0.17	7.2	9	31	4					140	166	140	112
1948	19	-1.8	Dover	ESHL	D	PHI	2	9	0.18	7.28	9.4	18						89	98	93	72
1948	19	-1.3	Bradford	PONY	D	PHI	1	6	0.14	7.06	8.29	13	4					51	68	47	40
1949	20	-0.8	Americus	GAFL	D	PHI	15	9	0.63	4.39	6	30						207	192	138	101
1950	21	-1.7	Wilmington	ISLG	B	PHI	12	4	0.75	3.71	5.06	26	23					153	147	86	63
1951	22	-2.5	Schenectady	EL	A	PHI	15	11	0.58	3.58	4.65	30	29					211	182	109	84
1952	23	-0.7	Schenectady	EL	A	PHI	16	8	0.67	2.94	3.73	35	24					205	189	85	67
1953	24	-3.3	Baltimore	IL	AAA	PHI	14	13	0.52	3.96	5.04	32	30		11	0		200	186	112	88
1954	25	-2.9	Syracuse	IL	AAA	PHI	8	14	0.36	3.86	4.56	28	24		6	2		154	142	78	66
Minors (7 seasons)					Minors		83	74	0.53	4.12	5.3	212	134		17	2		1270	1204	748	581
D (2 seasons)					Minors		18	24	0.43	5.52	7.21	61	4					347	358	278	213
A (2 seasons)					Minors		31	19	0.62	3.27	4.2	65	53					416	371	194	151
AAA (2 seasons)					Minors		22	27	0.45	3.92	4.83	60	54		17	2		354	328	190	154

Year	Age	AgeDif	Tm	Lg	Lev	Aff	HR	BB	IBB	SO	HBP	BK	WP	BF	WHIP	H9	HR9	BB9	SO9	SOW
1948	19		2 Teams	2 Lgs	D	PHI		134							2.14	11		8.6		
1948	19	-1.8	Dover	ESHL	D	PHI		97							2.19	9.9		9.8		
1948	19	-1.3	Bradford	PONY	D	PHI		37							2.06	12		6.5		
1949	20	-0.8	Americus	GAFL	D	PHI		135							1.58	8.3		5.9		
1950	21	-1.7	Wilmington	ISLG	B	PHI		113							1.7	8.6		6.6		
1951	22	-2.5	Schenectady	EL	A	PHI		125							1.46	7.8		5.3		
1952	23	-0.7	Schenectady	EL	A	PHI		91							1.37	8.3		4		
1953	24	-3.3	Baltimore	IL	AAA	PHI	11	110		128	5		9		1.48	8.4	0.5	5	5.8	1.16
1954	25	-2.9	Syracuse	IL	AAA	PHI	9	84		100	8		4		1.47	8.3	0.5	4.9	5.8	1.19
D (2 seasons)					Minors			269							1.81	9.3		7		
A (2 seasons)					Minors			216							1.41	8		4.7		
AAA (2 seasons)					Minors		20	194		228	13	2	13		1.48	8.3	0.5	4.9	5.8	1.18

Source: http://www.baseball-reference.com/register/player.cgi?id=sanfor003joh

Rookie of the Year Award Winners—NL and AL

| 1947 | Jackie Robinson, Dodgers | |
| 1948 | Al Dark, Braves | |

	NATIONAL LEAGUE	AMERICAN LEAGUE
1949	Don Newcombe, Dodgers	Roy Sievers, Browns
1950	Sam Jethroe, Braves	Walt Dropo, Red Sox
1951	Willie Mays, Giants	Gil McDougald, Yankees
1952	Joe Black, Dodgers	Harry Byrd, Athletics
1953	Jim Gilliam, Dodgers	Harvey Kuenn, Tigers
1954	Wally Moon, Cardinals	Bob Grim, Yankees
1955	Bill Virdon, Cardinals	Herb Score, Indians
1956	Frank Robinson, Reds	Luis Aparicio, White Sox
1957	**JACK SANFORD, Phillies**	Tony Kubek, Yankees
1958	Orlando Cepeda, Giants	Albie Pearson, Senators
1959	Willie McCovey, Giants	Bob Allison, Senators
1960	Frank Howard, Dodgers	Ron Hanson, Orioles
1961	Billy Williams, Cubs	Don Schwall, Red Sox
1962	Ken Hubbs, Cubs	Tom Tresh, Yankees
1963	Pete Rose, Reds	Gary Peters, White Sox
1964	Dick Allen, Phillies	Tony Oliva, Twins
1965	Jim Lefebvre, Dodgers	Curt Blefary, Orioles
1966	Tommy Helms, Reds	Tommie Agee, White Sox
1967	Tom Seaver, Mets	Rod Carew, Twins
1968	Johnny Bench, Reds	Stan Bahnsen, Yankees
1969	Ted Sizemore, Dodgers	Lou Pinella, Royals
1970	Carl Morton, Expos	Thurman Munson, Yankees
1971	Earl Williams, Braves	Chris Chambliss, Indians
1972	Jon Matlack, Mets	Carlton Fisk, Red Sox
1973	Gary Matthews, Giants	Al Bumbry, Orioles
1974	Bake McBride, Cardinals	Mike Hargrove, Rangers
1975	John Montefusco, Giants	Fred Lynn, Red Sox

162

1976	Butch Metzger, Padres	Mark Fidrych, Tigers
	Pat Zachry, Reds	
1977	Andre Dawson, Expos	Eddie Murray, Orioles
1978	Bob Horner, Braves	Lou Whitaker, Tigers
1979	Rick Sutcliffe, Dodgers	John Castino, Twins
		Alfredo Griffin, Blue Jays
1980	Steve Howe, Dodgers	Joe Charboneau, Indians
1981	Fernando Valenzuela, Dodgers	Dave Righetti, Yankees
1982	Steve Sax, Dodgers	Cal Ripken, Orioles
1983	Darryl Strawberry, Mets	Ron Kittle, White Sox
1984	Dwight Gooden, Mets	Alvin Davis, Mariners
1985	Vince Coleman, Cardinals	Ozzie Guillen, White Sox
1986	Todd Worrell, Cardinals	Jose Canseco, A's
1987	Benito Santiago, Padres	Mark McGwire, A's
1988	Chris Sabo, Reds	Walt Weiss, A's
1989	Jerome Walton, Cubs	Gregg Olson, Orioles
1990	David Justice, Braves	Sandy Alomar, Indians
1991	Jeff Bagwell, Astros	Chuck Knoblauch, Twins
1992	Eric Karros, Dodgers	Pat Listach, Brewers
1993	Mike Piazza, Dodgers	Tim Salmon, Angels
1994	Raul Mondesi, Dodgers	Bob Hamelin, Royals
1995	Hideo Nomo, Dodgers	Marty Cordova, Twins
1996	Todd Hollandsworth, Dodgers	Derek Jeter, Yankees
1997	Scott Rolen, Phillies	Nomar Garciaparra, Red Sox
1998	Kerry Wood, Cubs	Ben Grieve, A's
1999	Scott Williamson, Reds	Carlos Beltran, Royals
2000	Rafael Furcal, Braves	Kazuhiro Sasaki, Mariners
2001	Albert Pujols, Cardinals	Ichiro Suzuki, Mariners
2002	Jason Jennings, Rockies	Eric Hinski, Blue Jays
2003	Dontrelle Willis, Marlins	Angel Berroa, Royals
2004	Jason Bay, Pirates	Bobby Crosby, A's
2005	Ryan Howard, Phillies	Huston Street, A's
2006	Hanley Ramirez, Marlins	Justin Verlander, Tigers
2007	Ryan Braun, Brewers	Dustin Pedroia, Red Sox
2008	Geovany Soto, Cubs	Evan Longoria, Rays
2009	Chris Coghlan, Marlins	Andrew Bailey, A's

2010	Buster Posey, Giants	Neftali, Feliz, Rangers
2011	Craig Kimbrel, Braves	Jeremy Hellickson, Rays
2012	Bryce Harper, Nats	Mike Trout, Angels
2013	Jose Fernandez, Marlins	Wil Myers, Rays
2014	Jacob deGrom, Mets	Jose Abreu, White Sox

Source: http://www.baseball-reference.com/awards/roy_rol.shtml

About the Author

Jim Hawkins' award-winning career covering Major League Baseball has spanned half a century. He has written eight books, including biographies of Detroit Tigers Hall of Famer Al Kaline, Jack Sanford's Massachusetts hunting buddy Mark "The Bird" Fidrych, and ex-convict Ron LeFlore.

In 2013, he was nominated for the Baseball Hall of Fame's J.G. Taylor Spink Award, the highest honor that a baseball writer can receive. He is a member of Athletic and Academic Hall of Fame in his hometown of Superior, Wisconsin.

Although baseball is his specialty, he has also covered golf, including ten Masters tournaments and three Ryder Cups, football, including three Super Bowls, and auto racing, focusing on the Daytona 500 and Indianapolis 500.

During the course of his career, he has personally known dozens of Jack Sanford's former teammates and managers. A Giants fan at the time, Hawkins shared a bit of Jack's pain as he watched the fateful seventh game of the 1962 World Series in the student union at the University of Wisconsin.

CPSIA information can be obtained
at www.ICGtesting.com
Printed in the USA
BVOW08s1057121217
502579BV00001B/60/P